GREAT WRITERS OF THE ENGLISH LANGUAGE

Modern Novelists

STAFF CREDITS

Executive Editor
Reg Wright

Series Editor
Sue Lyon

Editors
Jude Welton
Sylvia Goulding

Deputy Editors
Alice Peebles
Theresa Donaghey

Features Editors
Geraldine McCaughrean
Emma Foa
Ian Chilvers

Art Editors
Kate Sprawson
Jonathan Alden
Helen James

Designers
Simon Wilder
Frank Landamore

Senior Picture Researchers
Julia Hanson
Vanessa Fletcher
Georgina Barker

Picture Clerk
Vanessa Cawley

Production Controllers
Judy Binning
Tom Helsby

Editorial Secretaries
Fiona Bowser
Sylvia Osborne

Managing Editor
Alan Ross

Editorial Consultant
Maggi McCormick

Publishing Manager
Robert Paulley

Reference Edition Published 1989
Published by Marshall Cavendish Corporation
147 West Merrick Road
Freeport, Long Island
N.Y. 11520

Typeset by Litho Link Ltd., Welshpool
Printed and Bound in Italy by
L.E.G.O. S.p.a. Vicenza

LIBRARY OF CONGRESS
Library of Congress Cataloging-in-Publication Data
Great Writers of the English Language
        p. cm.
        Includes index vol.
        ISBN 1-85435-000-5 (set): $399.95
        1. English literature — History and criticism. 2. English
literature — Stories, plots, etc. 3. American literature — History
and criticism. 4. American literature — Stories, plots, etc.
5. Authors. English — Biography. 6. Authors. American — Biography.
I. Marshall Cavendish Corporation.
PR85.G66 1989
820'.9 – dc19   88-21077
                                                                          CIP

ISBN 1–85435–000–5 (set)
ISBN 1–85435–006–4 (vol)

GREAT WRITERS OF THE ENGLISH LANGUAGE

Modern Novelists

D. H. Lawrence

Robert Graves

H. E. Bates

Graham Greene

MARSHALL CAVENDISH · NEW YORK · TORONTO · LONDON · SYDNEY

CONTENTS

D. H. LAWRENCE

The Writer's Life 6

Prophet or Pornographer?

Reader's Guide 12

*THE VIRGIN AND THE GIPSY
AND OTHER STORIES*

The Writer at Work 18

A Passionate Struggle

Sources & Inspiration 24

Mexican Magic

ROBERT GRAVES

The Writer's Life 30

In Search of a Muse

Reader's Guide 36

I, CLAUDIUS

The Writer at Work 42

Olympian Dreamer

Sources & Inspiration 48

Roman Gods and Heroes

H. E. BATES

The Writer's Life 54

A Rural Spirit

Reader's Guide 60

LOVE FOR LYDIA

The Writer at Work 66

Painting with Words

Sources & Inspiration 72

Changing Times

GRAHAM GREENE

The Writer's Life 78

Courting Danger

Reader's Guide 84

THE COMEDIANS

The Writer at Work 90

The Human Factor

Sources & Inspiration 96

Haiti – Nightmare Republic

BIBLIOGRAPHY 101

INDEX 102

D. H. LAWRENCE

1885 - 1930

D. H. Lawrence explored previously uncharted areas of human experience. His troubled boyhood and tempestuous marriage, his vulnerability to the powerful forces of sexual passion, all became the raw material of his art. His work outraged many and fell foul of the censors, and Lawrence abandoned England to wander the world in search of a better, truer way of life. He never found rest during his painfully brief career, but his quest enriched modern literature beyond measure.

PROPHET OR PORNOGRAPHER?

The critics called his books "sex depravity". His friends called him a visionary. Meanwhile, sick and restless, Lawrence took his burden of passion and talent in search of an earthly paradise.

With his working-class background and volatile, charismatic personality, D. H. Lawrence cut an unusual figure on the literary scene of the early 1900s. Hailed as a prophet by some and condemned as a pornographer by others, Lawrence was beset by controversy. His short, troubled life was one of stormy relationships and restless wanderings, scarred by bad health and illuminated by a supreme literary talent.

David Herbert Richards Lawrence was born on 11 September 1885 at Eastwood, a little mining town a few miles from Nottingham. His father, Arthur Lawrence, was a hearty, barely literate coal miner with a taste for alcohol that outraged his wife Lydia. Better educated than her husband, Lydia was determined that

none of her five children should go 'down t' pit'. Family life was full of rows and tensions, which left their mark on Lawrence and which he was to recapture vividly in one of his most famous novels, *Sons and Lovers*.

The future writer was the Lawrences' fourth child, 'a delicate pale brat with a snuffy nose' whose constitutional frailty was already apparent. His passion for nature and his preference for the company of girls puzzled the rough colliers' sons, but Bert Lawrence was a clever boy who did well enough at the local Board School to be entered for a scholarship to Nottingham High School. He won it – £12 a year – and became one of the very few working-class children to receive a secondary education.

At the end of three years at Nottingham High

Keith Sagar

End-of-terrace
The Lawrences paid an extra sixpence a week for the privilege of renting the end-of-terrace cottage in The Breach (above) in Eastwood. Although a coal miner's home, it was by no means squalid. Nevertheless, in retrospect, Lawrence found the surrounding industrial landscapes (below) soulless and inhuman – 'visions of pure ugliness'.

Charles Longbotham: Sunset and Industry. Victoria and Albert Museum/Bridgeman Art Library

Haggs, a smallholding three miles from Eastwood run by Edmund and Sarah Anne Chambers and their seven children. The happy atmosphere of the farm delighted him, and he fell in love with the whole family. For their part the Chambers brought out the best in Lawrence, whose helpfulness, lively responses and resourcefulness in inventing games brightened their existence. As Mr Chambers declared, 'Work goes like fun when Bert's there'. For several years the Haggs was a second home to Lawrence: 'a new life began in me there'.

TEACHING AND LEARNING

Lawrence never returned to clerking. In 1902 he became a pupil-teacher at the British School in Eastwood, taking classes while himself receiving instruction. After 'three years' teaching of savage collier lads' at £5 a year, he had passed enough examinations and saved enough money to take up a scholarship to Nottingham University College. Although he found college 'mere disillusion, instead of the living contact of men', he did emerge from it a qualified teacher.

Being a student gave Lawrence time for writing. Over the years at the Haggs he had grown very close to one of the Chambers girls, Jessie (the 'Miriam' of *Sons and Lovers*). He was later to describe their relationship as a 'betrothal of six years' standing', though its development was hindered by the jealous hostility of Lawrence's mother. With Jessie, he explored the world of literature, and her encouragement and enthusiasm was vital to his flowering as a writer.

It was this encouragement which was soon to be equally important in getting Lawrence published. In the autumn of 1908 he took up his first official teaching post, at Davidson Road School in Croydon. A few months later, Jessie copied

Family and friends
The conflict within the Lawrence family (left), with its imposingly handsome father and dauntingly ambitious matriarch, took its toll on Bert (pictured between his parents). He found sanctuary and friendship in the nearby home of Jessie Chambers (above). It was she who first encouraged him to be a writer.

'A damnable time'
Nottingham University College (below) did not live up to the young Lawrence's expectations. 'College gave me nothing,' he wrote, and he left there 'bitten . . . deep with disappointment'.

School, Lawrence, not yet 16, was found a job as a clerk with a surgical goods' firm in the city, and seemed set on a course that was unlikely to alter. But after three months he suffered a severe attack of pneumonia which brought him near to death. His mother, who had just lost her favourite son, nursed Bert devotedly, and a fiercely possessive bond was forged.

But Mrs Lawrence had a rival. As part of his convalescence, Lawrence started visiting the

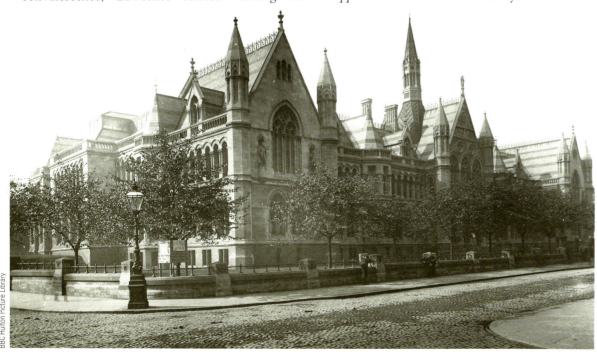

Key Dates

1885 born at Eastwood

1898 Nottingham High School

1906 Nottingham University College

1908 teacher in Croydon

1909 poems published in *English Review*

1910 mother dies

1911 *The White Peacock*

1912 meets Frieda

1922 visits Ceylon, New Mexico and Australia

1928 *Lady Chatterley's Lover* published in Florence

1930 dies at Vence

7

out and sent some of his poems to Ford Madox Hueffer, editor of *The English Review*. Hueffer, who had an exceptional flair for recognizing original work, published the poems in his magazine, helped Lawrence to place his first novel, *The White Peacock* published in 1911, and introduced him to London literary life. Lawrence's horizons were widening, though his emotional life was in some confusion – he was involved with Jessie, with another Eastwood woman, Alice Dax, with whom he probably had his first sexual experience, and with Helen Corke, a fellow-teacher at Croydon.

FRIEDA VON RICHTHOFEN

Lawrence's wife was six years older than him – a German aristocrat related to the World War I air ace Baron Manfred von Richthofen, 'the Red Baron'. Her marriage to lecturer Ernest Weekley lasted 12 years, and they had three children. But her provincial life bored her and she had already had several lovers when she met D. H. Lawrence. He wrote, 'She's got a figure like a fine Rubens woman, but her face is almost Greek.' It was he who insisted that an affair was not enough and that Frieda must run away with him. The cost was high: her wronged husband cut her off from her children. After Lawrence's death, Frieda became the lover of his friend John Middleton Murry and later married an Italian, Angelo Ravagli. She died in 1956.

In December 1910 Lawrence's mother died of cancer – a traumatic event that he sought to cope with, or escape from, by becoming engaged to Louie Burrows, 'a glorious girl ... swarthy and ruddy as a pomegranate', with whom he had been friendly since his pupil-teacher days. But 1911 was 'the sick year' – psychologically and eventually physically. In November Lawrence came down with pneumonia again and was told that he would become consumptive if he carried on teaching. The doctor's pronouncement gave him an excuse to break off his by now unwanted engagement, and force him to try his hand at being a full-time professional writer.

The culminating event of this critical period occurred in March 1912, while Lawrence was staying with his sister in Eastwood. He called on his old professor, Ernest Weekley, head of the Department of Modern Languages at Nottingham University College, and met Weekley's German wife, Frieda. Two months later Lawrence and Frieda eloped abroad, and in 1914, after Frieda's divorce, they were married. This was the central relationship of Lawrence's life, explored time and again in his writing. Frieda, a lazy and amoral aristocrat, was quite unlike Lawrence, and sturdily resisted his attempts to dominate or bully her – which was probably just what he needed. Despite infidelities, volcanic rows and furious throwing of plates, the relationship endured.

In 1912 Lawrence and Frieda went to Germany, walked over the Alps into Italy and wintered on Lake Garda. Lawrence was now writing hard, fully launched as a professional. He finished *Sons and Lovers*, which completed his break with Jessie; but more positively, its publication in 1913 brought him new friends in the literary world – most notably the critic John Middleton Murry and the New Zealand born short-story writer Katherine Mansfield, later Murry's wife.

A home in Italy
After a trip through Italy, the Lawrences took a villa in Sicily, at Taormina (above).

Close friendships
Relations between the Murrys (John Middleton Murry and Katherine Mansfield, below) and the Lawrences were intense. Murry resisted Frieda's advances, because of loyalty to his beloved 'Lorenzo', but was often critical of Lawrence's writing.

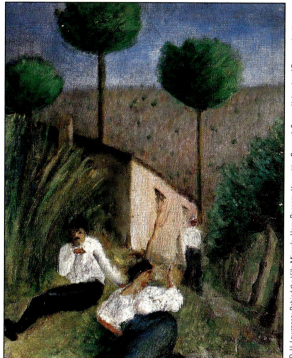

Most of Lawrence's friendships were fraught, but his relationship with Murry – that of hectoring master and unreliable chief disciple – was particularly strained and tortuous. Among others whom he met during this period were the patron-anthologist Edward Marsh, E.M. Forster, Lady Ottoline Morrell and the philosopher Bertrand Russell, over whom he exercised a remarkable, though temporary, influence.

A NIGHTMARE PERIOD

Newly married, Lawrence was on a walking tour of the Lake District when World War I broke out, trapping him and Frieda in England. Lawrence was quite obviously unfit to serve (though he was twice subjected to military medical examinations). He loathed the war, which he saw as the culmination of soulless mechanization, now applied to mass slaughter. This was a nightmare period, intensified by his first serious clash with British censorship. His novel *The Rainbow*, published in September 1915, was prosecuted for obscenity by the Public Morality Council; the publisher cravenly apologized, pleading that he was unaware of the book's contents, and with a few exceptions (Arnold Bennett was one) its suppression was effected without any protest whatsoever from the literary establishment.

Worse was to follow. The Lawrences settled at Zennor in Cornwall, where their bohemian ways and Frieda's German origin brought them under popular suspicion. The hysterical wartime mood was such that local people even believed the clothes on the Lawrences' washing line to be a semaphore signal intended for lurking U-boats. In 1917, after a police search of their cottage, they were given just three days to pack up and leave Cornwall for an unprohibited area, where they were required to report regularly to the police.

The war completed Lawrence's disenchantment with civilization, intensifying one of his recurrent waking dreams – to set up a colony of like-minded individuals, a utopian community which he named Rananim. In some distant place they could 'live out of the world – make a sort of Garden of Eden of blameless but fulfilled souls'. But when it came to the point, even his closest friends were not keen to leave England and live in too close proximity to a prickly genius such as Lawrence.

The Armistice of November 1918 ended the War, but soon afterwards Lawrence was laid low by the influenza epidemic that was sweeping the world. It was November 1919 before he was able to leave England, which was never again his home. He visited Florence and Capri, meeting the

Villa Mirenda
Lawrence rented the top floor of a hill-top villa in Tuscany for a year. He wrote and painted there – the above view of the Villa Mirenda is painted by him.

Tregarthen Cottage
(below) During the war, Lawrence and Frieda 'hibernated' in the Cornish countryside. But the locals mistrusted them and, branded as spies, the Lawrences were ordered to leave.

9

novelists Norman Douglas and Compton Mackenzie, before settling in a villa at Taormina in Sicily in March 1920.

Lawrence and Frieda spent two richly creative years at Taormina before his inveterate restlessness drove him to move again. Feeling that Europe was 'finished', he responded favourably to an invitation to Taos in New Mexico from Mabel Dodge Sterne, a much-married American who had set up an artists' colony there. One of its attractions was the local Indian culture; Lawrence was fascinated by primitive peoples, whose 'blood wisdom' seemed to him superior to Western man's 'head consciousness'.

But he was not sure that he would like the formidable Mrs Sterne, and put off a decision while he and Frieda took ship – in the opposite direction. They spent a few weeks at Colombo in Ceylon, enough time to convince Lawrence that he could not live in the tropics. Then they went on to Australia, where Lawrence exercised his uncanny gift for capturing the essence of a place almost at once.

In Western Australia Lawrence met Mollie Skinner, a sometime nurse and sometime novellist whose *The Boy in the Bush* he was later to revise and publish under their joint names. And during a few weeks spent at Thirroul, New South Wales, he wrote his next novel, *Kangaroo*. But Australia could not hold him, and in August 1922 he and Frieda left for San Francisco, Taos and Mabel Sterne.

ROCKY MOUNTAIN HOME

'Taos too much. Mabel Sterne and suppers and motor drives and people dropping in', Lawrence tersely noted of the artists' colony dominated by his hostess, whose designs on him amused and irritated Frieda. But New Mexico was 'the greatest experience from the outside world that I have ever had'. Here Lawrence learned to ride and, as soon as they could, he and Frieda moved out to 'an old brown log cabin' in the Rockies.

The following spring they crossed the border, staying in Mexico City and Chapala while Lawrence began his Mexican novel, *The Plumed Serpent*. But after 3 months they left for New York, intending to sail for England. Frieda was tired of the Mexican heat, and was longing to see her children, who had been kept away from her by her ex-husband but were now grown up. Lawrence went with reluctance ('my soul doesn't want to come to Europe'), and in New York he and Frieda quarrelled violently. Lawrence stayed behind, and for a time it seemed that the marriage was over.

Eventually it was Lawrence who came across the Atlantic to Frieda. But neither enjoyed Europe now, and Lawrence tried – unsuccessfully – to raise recruits to return with him to a New Mexican Rananim. Lawrence and Frieda sailed back to America in March 1924, accompanied on the *Aquitania* by a single disciple – the

Dorothy Brett
This young artist (right), fresh from an affair with John Middleton Murry, devoted herself to Lawrence. She followed him to New Mexico, and painted the above portrait in 1925. But Frieda told her to go, saying 'You are just a beastly nuisance.'

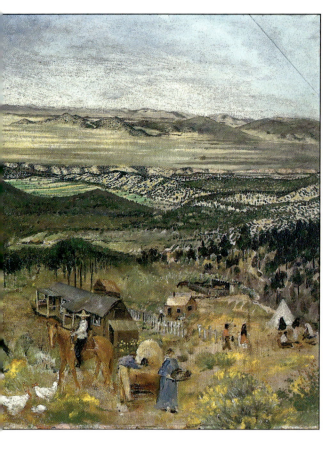

In a new world
'In the magnificent fierce morning of New Mexico one sprang awake . . . the old world gave way to a new,' wrote Lawrence, at first supremely happy in Mabel Sterne's desert community at Taos. He and Dorothy Brett painted and rode together. They both worked on the picture, left, of the ranch. The individual characters are all depictions of Lawrence, Frieda and Brett, occupied in various different daily tasks. But Frieda felt excluded by such intimate shared pastimes as painting.

down and destroy copies that had been imported surreptitiously.

Lawrence's notoriety was further increased when his paintings were exhibited at a London gallery in 1929. Twelve thousand people went to see them, including a group of policemen (sent by the Home Secretary) who removed 13 of the paintings. Lawrence's nudes, which now seem inoffensive enough, were judged obscene and narrowly escaped being burnt.

"NOT MUCH LEFT OF ME"

By this time, Lawrence was a dying man, having suffered a terrible lung haemorrhage in the summer of 1927. His friend Aldous Huxley described him as 'living by sheer force of will and by nothing else'. On 6 February 1930 Lawrence entered a sanatorium at Vence, in the South of France, where Huxley and H.G. Wells were among the well-wishers who came to see him. He left the sanatorium on 1 March, but died at the nearby Villa Robermond the following day with Frieda beside him.

Lawrence was buried at Vence, but in 1935 his ashes were removed to the Kiowa Ranch in New Mexico, where Frieda placed them in a specially built chapel crowned with Lawrence's personal symbol, the immortal, self-resurrecting, fabulous bird, the phoenix.

Honourable Dorothy Brett, a partially deaf, forceful young painter who sported short hair, trousers and an ear trumpet.

The threesome spent spring and summer at Taos and the 'log cabin', now re-named by Lawrence the Kiowa Ranch, which Mabel Sterne generously presented to Frieda. Then they went to Mexico so that Lawrence could finish *The Plumed Serpent* – a disastrous trip during which Frieda insisted on the over-appreciative Brett being sent packing and Lawrence fell desperately ill with malaria at Oaxaca. When he went for a medical examination in Mexico City, a doctor told Lawrence the unpleasant truth – he was consumptive.

In September 1925 Lawrence left the New World – as it turned out, for the last time. He felt 'queer and foreign' in England, and from now onwards lived mainly in Italy. Here he became fascinated by the half-lost civilization of the Etruscans, whom he idealized as a life-loving people destroyed by the power and money-hungry forces of the Romans, a favoured theme of his.

LADY CHATTERLEY

Until the last two years of his life Lawrence remained as prolific as ever, among other works producing no fewer than three versions of the novel *Lady Chatterley's Lover*, his most bluntly expressed advocacy of sexual fulfilment. The book was printed in Florence in 1928, since there was no question of publishing it in England, where vigorous attempts were made to hunt

Keith Sagar

'Goodbye Lorenzo'
'Like a bird we put him away, a few of us who loved him,' wrote Frieda of Lawrence's burial in Vence. Five years later, she and her new husband removed Lawrence's ashes to a chapel built for him at Taos (above), where the ashes were cemented in place to prevent Mabel Sterne stealing them.

<small>Fact or Fiction</small>

MABEL DODGE STERNE

Having buried one husband and divorced two more, Mabel married American Indian Tony Luhan and had predatory designs on Lawrence. Intelligent but spoiled, she liked to dispense largesse to an adoring retinue. She recognized herself as *The Woman Who Rode Away*, a woman who gives herself ritually into the hands of Indians.

THE VIRGIN AND THE GIPSY
AND OTHER STORIES

In these three stories selected from the collection, Lawrence turned to the issue that dominated his life and his imagination – the struggle between men and women to find a way of loving.

'I can only write what I feel pretty strongly about: and that, at present, is the relation between men and women.' So wrote Lawrence in 1913. This concern lies at the heart of much of his writing – but his short stories display the wealth and breadth of his vision. Apart from exploring the nature of sexual relationships, Lawrence also focuses on clashing cultures, social class, and the tensions and jealousies of family life. And with his unique ability to evoke scenes, atmosphere and emotion, he captures the complex nature of human relationships in all its forms.

THE VIRGIN AND THE GIPSY

One of Lawrence's longer tales, *The Virgin and the Gipsy* is also one of his best-known. It concerns life at the Papplewick rectory, and a family stagnating under the influence of a malign old grandmother. Ever since the mother, who "had made a great glow, a flow of life, like a swift and dangerous sun", ran off with a penniless young man, it is Mater, the grandmother, who rules the household with the "full weight of [her] dead old hand".

Outwardly, life there is solid and respectable, but the youngest daughter Yvette – who is most like her mother – strains against the "stifling" and "unbearable" atmosphere. Longing for excitement, she is ripe for any experience life may throw her way, the less conventional the better.

On a chance outing she has her fortune told by a gipsy woman, and finds herself powerfully drawn to the woman's husband, with his dark, "insolent gaze" and roughly handsome features. He is drawn to her, too, and fully sensible of the

F. C. B. Cadell: The White Lady/Fine Art Photographic Library

Youthful defiance
Yvette (right) chafes at "the whole stagnant, sewerage sort of life" of the rectory (far right). Having committed the unpardonable sin of talking back to her malevolent, all-powerful grandmother, she remains unrepentant. "Let's dress ourselves up", she urges her sister, "and sail down to dinner like duchesses."

Sir Alfred Munnings: The Green Caravan. © The Sir Alfred Munnings Art Museum, Dedham, Essex

Gipsy life
Yvette's "soul had the half painful, half easing knack of leaving her, and straying away to some place, to somebody that had caught her imagination." After her first chance encounter, her mind often wandered back to the gipsies and their fresh outdoor life – "she felt intensely that that was home for her: the gipsy camp, the fire, the stool, the man with the hammer, the old crone."

12

> *"The gipsy man at the top of the steps stood imperturbable, without any expression at all. But his bold eyes kept staring at Yvette, she could feel them on her cheek, on her neck, and she dared not look up."*

THE WOMAN WHO RODE AWAY

Set in the Chihuahua mountains of Mexico, the story also tells of a woman in search of adventure, but the focus here is mystical rather than sexual. The "woman who rode away" is an American who has married a Dutch mine owner much older than herself, because she thought life with him would be an adventure. Instead, she finds herself trapped in a perfect little house from which she can see no escape.

On impulse, she decides to break free from her world and sets off on a journey into the mountains, to find an unknown Indian tribe. Almost at once she feels

power he has over her. A spark is lit between them, to be rekindled at subsequent meetings.

On their next encounter, the gipsy makes an assignation to meet at his caravan in his wife's absence. The development of the relationship is thwarted, however, and Yvette's final meeting with the gipsy seems all too likely to be the last for both of them as they are caught up in the flood waters of a dam burst.

The Virgin and the Gipsy is a compelling tale of a young girl's growth into womanhood and her desire to break free from what she feels to be the restricting conventions of her time. Yvette's development and the awakening of her sexual desire are inextricably linked with the conflict in her family life.

To Yvette, the gipsy represents the antithesis of rectory life, and therefore a potential escape from it. She sees purity in the gipsy's open-air, nomadic way of life, in contrast with her "awful, smelly family that would never disperse, stuck half dead around the base of a fungoid old woman!"

The bursting of the dam is both a climax and catalyst in the story. It obliterates the stifling and stagnant life of the

rectory and releases Yvette from the evil influence of her grandmother. Saved from the floods by the gipsy, events occur that propel her irrevocably forward. As the waters finally subside, Yvette, like the gipsy, has moved on, never to return.

In the Background

CENSORSHIP

When *The Rainbow* was published in 1915, it was attacked as 'a mass of obscenity of thought, idea and action'. Lawrence was a marked man after this: he could not find a publisher for *Women in Love* (completed in 1916 but not published until 1920, and then only in America); and even his paintings, exhibited in London in 1929, were seized by Scotland Yard and nearly destroyed.

In spite of this, Lawrence remained true to his values and to his art. In *Lady Chatterley's Lover* he described lovemaking with what was deemed unacceptable honesty. The result was that the novel could not be published in Britain until 1960 – a full 30 years after Lawrence's death.

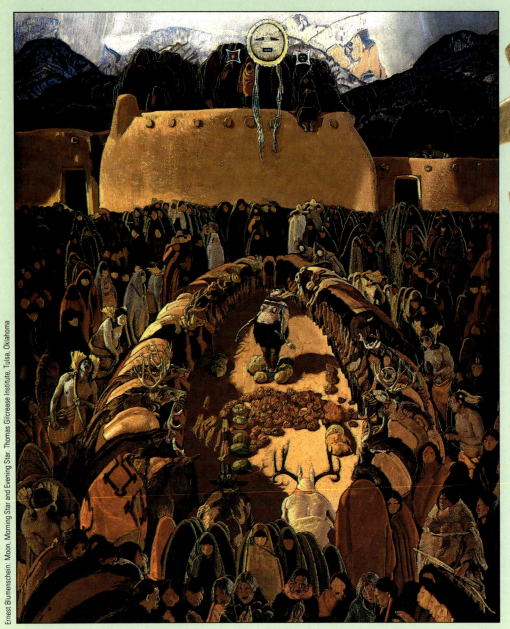

Ernest Blumenschein: Moon, Morning Star and Evening Star; Thomas Gilcrease Institute, Tulsa, Oklahoma

"Savage customs"
Intrigued by the "timeless, mysterious, marvellous Indians" living in the Mexican mountains, the "woman who rode away" (left) wants to penetrate, however briefly, their "savage customs and religion" (far left). But the experience turns out to be not so brief . . .

possibility of a mutually satisfactory relationship with a man. However, he also believed that a woman should not just submit to a man, but to something greater in the universe, and he accorded women distinct and special powers. If civilization were to be healed it could only do so by power returning to male hands in the ancient, traditional manner.

> *"She felt it was her destiny to wander into the secret haunts of these timeless, mysterious, marvellous Indians of the mountains."*

changed – her will drains away and she is seized by a sense of inertia. She journeys on, but "if she had had any will of her own left, she would have turned back … to be protected and sent home to her husband." Instead she entrusts her life and her destiny to some Chilchui Indians, and finds herself an honoured captive in their midst. For the most part she feels no fear, only a "cold, watchful wonder" which sustains her to the very end.

This tale is something of a departure for Lawrence and dates from the time when, reacting to the excesses of Western civilization, he went to live in Mexico.

The woman has no name because her identity is irrelevant – she is a symbol, caught up in what Lawrence saw as the sickness of Western civilization, surrounded by a strange and powerful Nature. As a white woman is needed in

order for the moon to "come down among the Indian women, like a white goat among the flowers", to restore power to the male Chilchui Indians, so civilization as it stands must be destroyed in order that something new and good can be reborn in its place.

The woman passes from one form of male domination in marriage to another form in the hands of the Chilchui and accepts this new role passively, with only occasional "shocks of fear". Her existence as a symbol, rather than as a woman, is underlined by the fact that the Indians do not see her as a sexual being at all – her nakedness leaves them unmoved.

Another theme running through the story requires some understanding of Lawrence's complex views regarding women's roles. By asserting their independence, he felt women jeopardized the

THE FOX
In *The Fox*, Lawrence pursues the question of mastery using the device of a triangle – one man and two women. In this tale, two young women, Banford and March, live on a farm. Banford is the weaker in health and plays the more feminine role, as homemaker. March strides around in jodhpurs or a man's coat and does much of the harder physical work. The implication is not so much of a lesbian relationship as of role-playing, and this starts to founder as the farm's fortunes decline.

The fox that is running off with their hens starts to obsess March, and she pits her intellect and energy against him. Yet when she has an opportunity to shoot him, she finds she is unable to do so – she feels spellbound by the animal's power over her.

When Henry Grenfel, the farm's previous owner's grandson, turns up unexpectedly, March is spellbound again – to her he is the embodiment of the fox, and she wants both to get away from him and submit to his presence. He offers her an escape from the intensity of her relationship with Banford – they have been "living too much off themselves". March is lured by the offer and Banford turns against him.

The Fox is essentially a love story, but in true Lawrentian style it is not a straightforward one. The two lovers find it difficult to acknowledge that they are in love, or even to recognize it as such. Henry first thinks of marrying March as a way of obtaining the farm – but before long, "He wanted the woman, he had fixed like doom upon having her. He felt that was his doom, his destiny and his reward … She was his heaven and hell on earth." He hardly realizes that the fascination he feels for her is love, for he has had little previous experience of it. Likewise, March is aware of the peace she feels in his company, without understanding why. She is as if robbed of her will by Henry's

> *"He chafed, feeling he hadn't got his own life. He would never have it till she yielded and slept in him. Then he would have all his own life as a young man and a male, and she would have all her own life as a woman and a female."*

presence, so that he must make all her decisions for her.

Yet, in her unconscious, March acknowledges what is happening, expressing it in her prophetic dreams. After her first meeting with Henry she dreams of an encounter with the fox in which his brush sears her mouth. Her first kiss with Henry is "a quick, brushing kiss" which seems to "burn through her every fibre". Her second dream is of Banford's death and suggests a kind of complicity in what is to follow – she does not want to lose Banford but at some level recognizes that she must if she is to marry Henry.

Once Henry begins to respond to his need for March, then the theme of man as predator begins to develop, and Henry realizes that to win March he must use a huntsman's wiles. His courtship is a "subtle, profound battle of wills which takes place in the invisible".

There is to be no happy or easy ending for March and Henry. March wants to retain some of her independence: "She *would* have the reins of her own life between her own hands. She *would* be an independent woman to the last." Henry, instead, wants her to yield to him. Unless one or both parties can make the effort of will required to get beyond the deadlock, Lawrence sees such partnership as doomed to be unhappy. And even if one party does submit to the other, the result is in no way assured – that, according to Lawrence, "is *the* problem of today".

Harald-Slott Muller: Feeding Ducks/Fine Art Photographic Library

Male predators
Having bought Bailey Farm (left), two young women, Banford and March, struggle to make a go of it by rearing chickens, ducks and heifers. But it is a continuing battle as predators – first fox, then man – threaten their livelihood and their partnership. March sets out to shoot the fox, but his cunning proves greater than hers and she finds herself somehow "possessed by him", feeling the fox "invisibly master her spirit". When a young soldier turns up at their door, "to March he was the fox" and she is similarly spellbound by him, sensing danger but powerless to save herself.

John Davis: The Fox in Winter (detail), Asser Fine Arts/Bridgeman Art Library

CHARACTERS IN FOCUS

The characters who people Lawrence's tales have both passionate intensity and subtle depths. Often their descriptions provide a key to their complex thoughts and emotions. The fact that they are frequently in conflict – both within themselves and within their intense relationships – is central to Lawrence's literary statement on the nature of the human condition.

WHO'S WHO
THE VIRGIN AND THE GIPSY

Yvette "With her fine, delicate flesh", Yvette is free-spirited but also selfish and naïve.

The Gipsy Unnamed until the very end, he is a powerful and insinuating presence.

Granny Yvette's grandmother – who is "like some awful idol of old flesh".

THE WOMAN WHO RODE AWAY

The Woman Virtually extinguished by her husband's adoration, she remains nameless throughout, not so much a character as a symbol.

The Young Indian The only other character of any substance, he explains the ways of the Chilchui to the white woman.

THE FOX

March Looking "almost like some graceful, loose-balanced young man", she is a vigorous young woman who shoulders "four-fifths of the work" on the farm, which she shares with her friend.

Banford "A thin, frail little thing" with a "worn face", she grows jealous as March becomes increasingly involved with the newcomer Henry.

Henry A young soldier just returned from Canada, who reminds March of the fox, with his "rather wide, cat-shaped face" and "bright keen eyes".

Andrew Wheatcroft

THE VIRGIN AND THE GIPSY

"A dandy, in his polished black boots, tight black trousers and tight dark green jersey", the gipsy (left) looks at Yvette with "the naked insinuation of desire" in his "dark, conceited proud eyes". He lives always outside society, an outcast, "too much master of himself and too wary to expose himself openly". But when he is needed most, he is there.

THE WOMAN WHO RODE AWAY

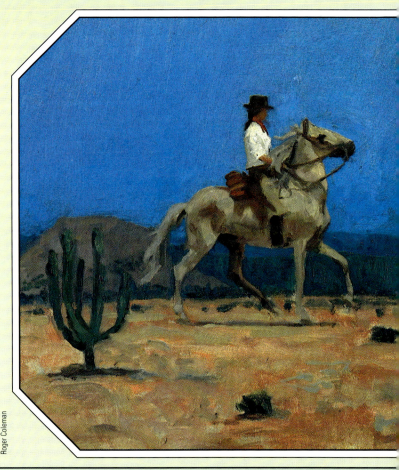

"Now thirty three, a large, blue-eyed dazed woman, beginning to grow stout", the "woman who rode away" (right) is "admired to extinction" by her husband, but has no sexual impact whatsoever on the Chilchui Indians she meets in the mountains. More a vehicle for Lawrence's mysticism than for characterization, she remains a nameless, undefined figure throughout. Her role, in the Chilchui scheme of things, is to "begin to make the world again" by the awesome ritual she knows she must undergo.

Roger Coleman

"Truly irritable and outrageously rude", **Yvette** (below) is bored by her surroundings, by Church duties and by the worthy but deadly dull young men she meets. She feels "a great, sardonic female contempt, for such domesticated dogs, calling themselves men", and when she meets the gipsy, "Something took fire within her breast . . . the surface of her body seemed to turn to water." Like a "bold, tall, young sloop, slipping from harbour", she feels life just beginning, and Nature herself takes a hand in freeing her . . .

Pierre Franc Lamy: Reclining Nude/Fine Art Photographic Library

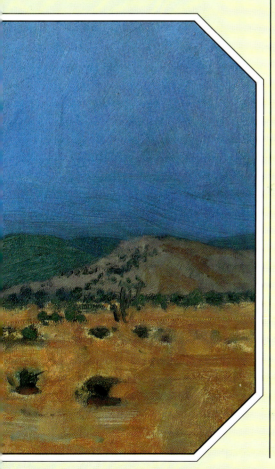

Richard Hook

THE FOX

March fascinates the young soldier who comes to the farm (above), but he knows that "he would have to catch her as you catch a deer or a woodcock when you go out shooting". And he engages in a "subtle, profound battle of wills", setting out to take her unawares, with all the stealth of his fox-like character.

A "warm, generous soul", Banford (left) welcomes the arrival of Henry Grenfel, listening to him "full of perky interest, like a bird". But their relationship soon deteriorates as she senses his predatory attitude towards March.

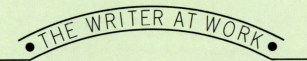

A PASSIONATE STRUGGLE

Throughout his life Lawrence battled against incomprehension and suppression of his work. But he remained true to his task of restoring real human values to an over–civilized age.

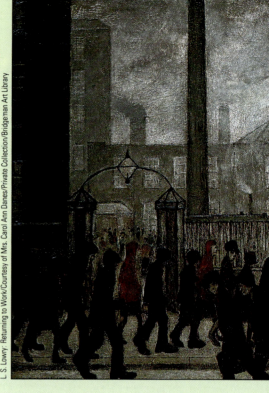

'I am a slow writer, really – I only have great outbursts of work', D. H. Lawrence told Edward Garnett, his chief literary adviser between the years 1911 and about 1915. The results of Lawrence's 'great outbursts' were extraordinary: 10 novels, dozens of short stories (some have been classified as short novels), over 900 poems, a handful of plays, four travel books, several volume-length collections of essays and critical works, a history textbook, thousands of vividly written letters, and quantities of magazine and newspaper articles – all done by a man who died when he was

The Rainbow made it impossible to find a publisher for *Women in Love,* and Lawrence's damaged reputation restricted the outlets for his fiction. In order to make some money he wrote a textbook, *Movements in Modern History* (published under the pseudonym of Lawrence H. Davison in 1921), and his most influential critical work, *Studies in Classic American Literature* (1923). Americans were more appreciative of Lawrence's work than his fellow-countrymen, and his US sales made life much easier for him during the 1920s. Towards the end of his life he was not above exploiting the renewed notori-

Crucial meeting
Lawrence's life with Frieda Weekley, the wife of his tutor and daughter of aristocratic German parents (left), gave new impetus to his writing.

Working-class background
(above) Lawrence grew up in the industrial Midlands. His consciousness of the effects of class and money permeates much of his writing.

only 44. To the list can be added a novel rewritten by Lawrence (Mollie Skinner's Australian tale, *The Boy in the Bush)* and a long unfinished novel, *Mr Noon,* only published in full in 1984.

As this indicates, Lawrence was a professional writer (his ill health made it impossible for him to take up any other profession). For years his income was very small – dependent on his reviews, essays and short stories – and he and Frieda lived very simply in little cottages where Lawrence did the housework.

Their lowest point was probably during World War I, when the suppression of

ety brought about by *Lady Chatterley's Lover,* and made money by contributing autobiographical sketches to the *Sunday Dispatch* and the *Evening News.* At his death Lawrence left over £4000, a very respectable sum in 1930.

But, for all his professionalism, Lawrence always wrote in his distinctive style, making no significant concessions to his readers. Indeed, by his own account he never allowed himself to think about his readers: 'One writes ... to some mysterious presence in the air. If that presence were not there, and one thought of even a single solitary actual

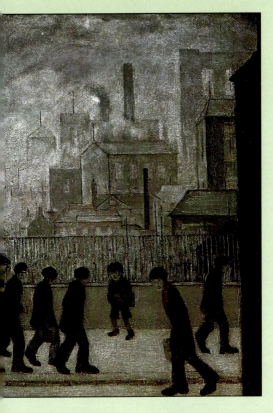

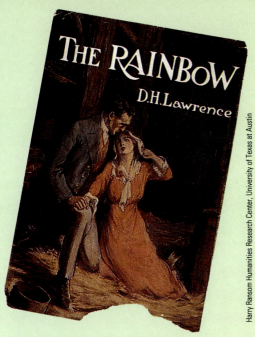

THE RAINBOW
D.H.Lawrence

Obscenity charges
(right) The cover of Lawrence's fourth novel hints at the passions contained within. On publication it was seized by the police.

reader, the paper would remain white for ever.' And, despite literary persecution, he continued writing to this 'unseen witness'.

EXCEPTIONAL WRITING

The exceptional quality of all his writing has meant that Lawrence's admirers have never been able to agree as to which literary medium suited him best. His poetry, though occasionally composed in a spiky, satirical vein, gives the purest expression to Lawrence's 'blood-affinity' with flowers and animals, which are perceived with a nervous intensity of self-identification found in no other author. Sombre late masterpieces such as *Bavarian Gentians* and *The Ship of Death* (in *Last Poems,* 1929) show him gaining in poetic authority towards the end of his life.

His earlier novels cost Lawrence a great deal of effort. It took four years to turn a first draft called *Laetitia* into *The White Peacock* (1911); three to change *Paul Morel* into *Sons and Lovers* (1913), which Edward Garnett pruned by about a tenth before publication. *The Sisters* became first *The Wedding Ring* and eventually two novels, *The Rainbow* (1915) and *Women in Love* (1920); in April 1914 Lawrence complained, 'Oh, I tried so hard to work, this last year. I began a novel seven times. I have written a thousand pages I shall burn. But ... I have done two-thirds.'

SPEED AND FLUENCY

Lawrence evidently wrote extremely quickly, but was prepared to scrap what he had done and try again to get exactly the effect he wanted. This was still true of his last novel, *Lady Chatterley's Lover* (1928): between October 1926 and January 1928 he wrote no less than three versions, as well as vainly attempting to produce an expurgated text acceptable to British and American publishers. By contrast, *Kangaroo* was finished in six weeks (despite the fact that Lawrence got stuck in the middle!), and two eight-week drafts became the very long *The Plumed Serpent*.

The clue to this remarkable fluency is that Lawrence wrote out of deeply felt personal experiences and observations. Apart from his capacity for responding freshly to places and people, he had amazingly accurate powers of recall, as when he spent a few days on the island of Sardinia with Frieda – without taking a single note – and afterwards wrote up their wanderings in one of his best travel books, *Sea and Sardinia* (1921). Throughout his writing career, until *Lady Chatterley's Lover,* Lawrence drew again and again on his early life in Eastwood and the surrounding countryside ('the country of my heart' as he called it), as well as on his foreign travels.

In Australia
(below) In 1922 Lawrence and Frieda visited Australia. Lawrence wrote the novel Kangaroo *there and also collaborated on* The Boy in the Bush.

Intellectual friendships
The patron Lady Ottoline Morrell and the philosopher Bertrand Russell (seen together right) were among Lawrence's friends.

Lawrence's shorter works of fiction have been given first place by many critics, who claim that his stories convey all his essential perceptions while avoiding the moodiness and tendency to preaching that sometimes mar his novels. However, Lawrence himself believed that the novel in general – not just his own novels – mattered supremely: it was 'the one bright book of life', the only medium in which the writer could present life in its entirety rather than in fragments. For Lawrence this was a moral rather than an artistic advantage: he believed that 'the novel can help us to live'.

On a deeper level, Lawrence's relationship with his wife Frieda – a German aristocrat – certainly coloured his view of sex as a force transcending class and nationality, a theme that occurs in many of the novels and with equal persistence in such shorter works of fiction as *The Captain's Doll, The Virgin and the Gipsy* and *The Daughters of the Vicar.*

Frieda's family background supplied the German military milieu of *The Prussian Officer,* and her own experiences as a young woman are reworked for some of Ursula's adventures in *The Rainbow.* And Frieda's fierce resistance to Lawrence's attempts to dominate her provided abundant material for the ever-present male-female struggle in his books, a resistance which complicated the already difficult task of forming satisfactory relationships in an unsatisfactory world.

UNCONSCIOUS FORCES

Lawrence treats the struggle between the sexes in a number of different ways: in *The Captain's Doll* he is keenly aware of the ludicrous aspect of male pretensions, whereas *The Plumed Serpent* and *The Woman Who Rode Away* imply a radical subduing of the female will through the return to primitivism – a solution to modern ills that intermittently appealed to Lawrence, although he finally rejected it.

In spite of the fact that much of Lawrence's material was grounded in reality – so much so that he was on several occasions threatened with libel actions –

Author-illustrator
Lawrence painted this frontispiece for his book The Escaped Cock, *a story about Christ after the Resurrection.*

Mexican inspiration
Lawrence led a nomadic life, but said that of all the places he visited 'I like Mexico best . . . to live in'; in Oaxaca, where he is seen below left, the climate was 'perfect'. Mexico, its spirit and ancient culture, were the inspiration for The Plumed Serpent, *as well as for stories and travel writing.*

The British Library, London

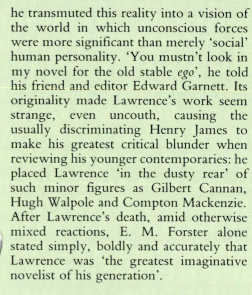

he transmuted this reality into a vision of the world in which unconscious forces were more significant than merely 'social' human personality. 'You mustn't look in my novel for the old stable *ego*', he told his friend and editor Edward Garnett. Its originality made Lawrence's work seem strange, even uncouth, causing the usually discriminating Henry James to make his greatest critical blunder when reviewing his younger contemporaries: he placed Lawrence 'in the dusty rear' of such minor figures as Gilbert Cannan, Hugh Walpole and Compton Mackenzie. After Lawrence's death, amid otherwise mixed reactions, E. M. Forster alone stated simply, boldly and accurately that Lawrence was 'the greatest imaginative novelist of his generation'.

LATTERDAY RECOGNITION

It was not until the 1950s that Forster's view began to be endorsed by other leading critics, F. R. Leavis's book *D. H. Lawrence, Novelist* (1955) being the most important work in the swing of taste. Lawrence's present great fame still rests mainly on the quality that brought him notoriety in his lifetime – his outspoken treatment of sex. He is indeed still sometimes accused of being unhealthily obsessed with sex. However, his writing is equally memorable for other qualities, not least his descriptions of the natural world, and for his extraordinary ability to recreate the people and places he knew throughout his wandering restless life.

BBC Hulton Picture Library

WORKS·IN OUTLINE

A prolific poet, short-story writer and novelist, D. H. Lawrence drew heavily on his own experience to portray the difficulty of living and loving naturally in an increasingly mechanistic and artificial world. His first novel, *The White Peacock* (1911), with its rural setting, revealed Lawrence's extraordinary powers of description. *Sons and Lovers* (1913) is a classic recollection of family life and growing up. *The Rainbow* (1915) and *Women in Love* (1920) constitute his most profound explorations of sexual relationships, contrasting with the passionate, violent primitivism of *The Plumed Serpent* (1926). But in *Lady Chatterley's Lover* (1928), written and reworked several times as he neared death, Lawrence reaffirmed the truth he had discovered within his own married life – the central importance of sexual love and tenderness to the fulfilment of man and woman alike.

THE WHITE PEACOCK

1911

The presence of a peacock (far left) – a readily understood symbol of vanity and pride – serves to underline the attention-seeking behaviour of the book's heroine, Lettie Beardsall (left). The narrator is Cyril Beardsall, a rather priggish, Lawrence-like young man whose sister Lettie is attracted to George Saxton, her neighbour. Saxton is handsome and manly, but too earthbound and sluggish to make the most of his chances with Lettie. She flirts with him, taunts him, makes fast her hold on him, then makes a 'prudent' match with the heir of a rich mine-owner. The disappointed George subsequently marries a warm but narrow, ignorant woman. These wrong choices lead to frustration and unhappiness. Lettie becomes an unfulfilled dabbler in the arts, living for and through her children. George sets out on a more openly ruinous course. The lyrical descriptions of the Nottinghamshire countryside setting relieve this increasingly painful story of thwarted human aspirations.

SONS AND LOVERS
1913

A promising young love (right) blighted by a misguided upbringing is the theme of this most directly autobiographical of Lawrence's novels. The main characters and the events that shape their lives are modelled on Lawrence's own childhood and young manhood. Throughout the novel's genesis, Lawrence showed sections of the manuscript to his friend and neighbour Jessie Chambers, the flesh-and-blood counterpart of the fictional Miriam Leivers in *Sons and Lovers,* and incorporated a number of her suggestions into the final version. In the novel, Gertrude Coppard, an ex-schoolteacher, has married Walter Morel, a handsome collier with an engagingly warm personality. But Gertrude is soon disillusioned by her husband's coarseness and addiction to drink, and lavishes all her love on her sons, with crippling effects on their ability to form satisfactory relationships with other women. After the death of his older brother, the second son, Paul, becomes the object of his mother's fiercely possessive affection (just as Lawrence was doted on after the death of *his* brother). Then Paul becomes friendly with the Leivers family at nearby Willey Farm, and is drawn to the shy, serious Miriam Leivers. She encourages him to become an artist. But her 'spiritual' love fails to satisfy him and he turns to a married woman, Clara Dawes, with whom he achieves physical fulfilment at last. The relationship ends when Clara returns to her husband. Mrs Morel becomes ill with cancer, and Paul and his sister, unable to bear her suffering, give her an overdose of morphine. Grief-stricken, Paul must now decide whether to follow his mother into 'the darkness', or choose life in spite of its tragedies.

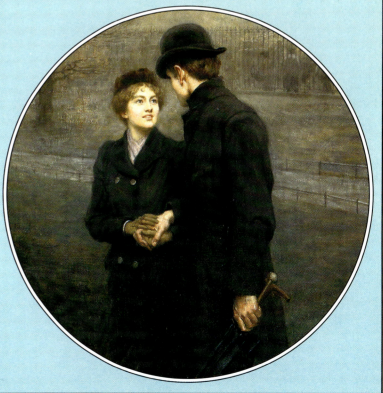

WOMEN IN LOVE

◆ 1920 ◆

The frigidity of Alpine Snow (right) finally extinguishes the passionate heat of a love affair in this sequel to *The Rainbow*. Ursula Brangwen and her sister Gudrun have become teachers in the mining town of Beldover. Ursula falls in love with Rupert Birkin, a school inspector, while Gudrun becomes involved with Rupert's friend, Gerald Crich, the mine-owner's son. Ursula and Rupert struggle through to a true partnership and marry, although Ursula fails to understand Rupert's conviction that a different kind of love, between men, is necessary for complete fulfilment (the relationship between him and Gerald is most powerfully expressed in a scene where they wrestle together). Meanwhile Gerald, put in charge of the colliery, introduces an efficient but soulless regime. His obstinate personality stops him responding to Rupert's attempts to establish a bond between them, and his entanglement with Gudrun is a destructive war of wills. When the couples take a holiday together, one of the relationships comes to a tragic end.

Like many of Lawrence's books, *Women in Love* caused a storm. Lawrence had difficulties getting it published, and it was condemned as obscene and court actions followed. However, Lawrence always maintained that it was his finest novel.

Sir E. A. Waterlow: Chalet in the Snow. Fine Art Society, London/Bridgeman Art Library

Renoir: After the Bath. Private Collection/Bridgeman Art Library

THE RAINBOW

◆ 1915 ◆

A brief lesbian affair (left) is one of the many aspects of sexuality treated in this saga about the Brangwen family. The novel follows the emotional history of three generations of Brangwens, a family long settled at Marsh Farm, close to the Nottinghamshire-Derbyshire border. Tom Brangwen falls in love with a Polish widow, Lydia Lensky. They marry and have two sons, but Tom's favourite is Anna, Lydia's child by her first husband. Tom reluctantly allows Anna to marry his nephew, Will Brangwen. Things are more difficult for the next generation – for Will and Anna's daughter, Ursula. Ultimately unsatisfied by her brief affair with a female teacher she becomes involved with the dashing Anton Skrebensky. Their battles over the question of love and marriage are fought out to an unconventional conclusion.

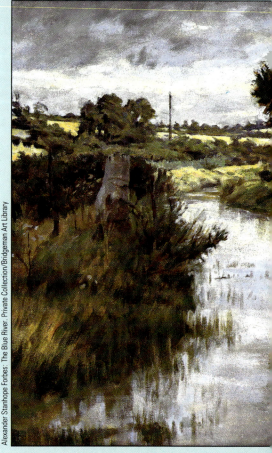

Alexander Stanhope Forbes: The Blue River. Private Collection/Bridgeman Art Library

THE PLUMED SERPENT

✦ 1926 ✦

The myths and images of Mexico (right) imbue this novel with the 'blood vigour' and magic which inspired Lawrence. Kate Leslie, an independent, 'modern' Irishwoman, is tired of husbands and lovers and disillusioned with European values. A compulsive traveller, she arrives in Mexico and finds it no better than anywhere else – until she meets the mystic and revolutionary Don Ramon Carrasco and his fanatical follower, General Cipriano. She becomes involved in their plan to renew Mexico by reviving the country's ancient religion: at its head, Don Ramon personifies the god Quetzalcoatl, the plumed serpent, while Cipriano represents the war-god Huitzilopochtli. Kate is both horrified and fascinated by the blood sacrifices performed in the name of the new cult, which spreads all over Mexico and becomes the official religion. In spite of her doubts, she accepts a place in the new Mexican pantheon as Malintzi, bride of Huitzilopochtli. They are married, even though Kate knows that the new order will require obedience and subordination from her, both socially and sexually. One of the more mystical of Lawrence's novels, it deals with the clash of ancient and modern cultures, and questions whether the 'modern' woman can survive such a role.

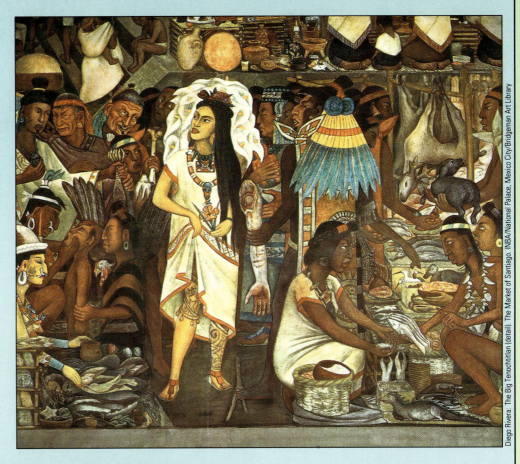

Diego Rivera: The Big Tenochtitlan (detail). The Market of Santiago. INBA/National Palace, Mexico City/Bridgeman Art Library

LADY CHATTERLEY'S LOVER

✦ 1928 ✦

Constance 'Connie' Chatterley (left) is married to mine-owner Sir Clifford Chatterley. Wounded in World War I, he has been left paralyzed from the waist downwards. He is willing for her to take a lover and bear him a child so as to continue the Chatterley line. But after one unsatisfactory affair, Connie makes love with her husband's gamekeeper, Oliver Mellors (far left). He is a man who carefully hides his complex and sensitive personality – and who is associated with Nature and the yearly round of life and death. Although by no means sexually inexperienced, Connie finds in Mellors a sexual spontaneity and tenderness she has never known. She becomes pregnant, to the indignation of Sir Clifford, whose tolerance evaporates in the face of class prejudice. Through all the ensuing complications, the lovers look forward hopefully to a life together.

 The chief cause for the novel's notoriety was Lawrence's attempt to rehabilitate certain four-letter words by using them freely in scenes of sexual tenderness. As a result, British readers were not permitted to buy an unexpurgated edition of the book until 1960.

E. K. Johnson: Quiet/Fine Art Photographic Library

MEXICAN MAGIC

Chichén Itzá
The sacred city of Chichén Itzá (below) was the largest centre of Toltec and Mayan civilization. The stepped pyramid was dedicated to Quetzalcoatl, the Plumed Serpent, and serpent imagery in all its forms permeates Mexican culture. The duality between opposed forces, as personified by the Mexican gods, had an irresistible appeal to Lawrence.

'The Indian, the Aztec, old Mexico – all that fascinates me and has fascinated me for years. *There* is glamour and magic for me . . . It seems to me my fate.' D. H. LAWRENCE

When D. H. Lawrence visited Mexico in 1923 it captured his imagination as no other country had done or would do. It intrigued and mystified him. It had one reality on the surface and quite another within, and though Lawrence was captivated by both, loving the surface colour, the "brilliant sun . . .

Ancient and modern
The Indians were steeped in ritual and mythology, incorporating many ancient beliefs into their own mystical view of life. The carving of the priest (right) dates from around AD *700 and yet has strikingly similar facial features to those of the modern Indian (left).*

sented the sort of instinctive life force that Lawrence explored and celebrated in much of his writing.

The Indian population of ancient Mexico was made up of many different tribes and, as Lawrence noted in *The Plumed Serpent,* that variety was still evident in their modern-day descen-

on the hibiscus flowers . . . the fluttering yellow and green rags of the banana trees", it was the inner aspect of Mexico, with its darkly mystical people and places, that crept inside him, lodging itself somewhere deep within his being.

GREATER TRUTHS

Throughout his young manhood, Lawrence had been somehow dissatisfied with his surroundings, searching for a greater truth, something to give meaning to the form of everyday things. And Mexico seemed to provide, if not the answer, then certainly a key. The local Indians, with their mixture of magic and ritual, their dances, their closeness to Nature, inspired Lawrence to try to penetrate their 'blood consciousness' and learn the secrets of their ancient, timeless religion. And in the relics of the past – the pyramids and the temples – lay clues to the various civilizations that had tamed and shaped present-day Mexico.

The temples honoured and reflected ancient deities – Aztec, Mayan and Toltec – that were all interlinked. The most celebrated of these deities, Quetzalcoatl, the Plumed Serpent, fascinated Lawrence beyond all the others. Seen all over Mexico in different forms, this deity repre-

dants, from the "wild, sombre, erect men of the north" to the "quick little Indians, quick as spiders, down in Oaxaca" and the "half-Chinese natives towards Vera Cruz". In Quetzalcoatl they shared a common deity, though their cultural practices and methods of worship differed over time and region.

Like King Arthur, Quetzalcoatl is half-man, half-legend. His historical existence is not disputed, though there is little hard fact to go on. At some time in history – whether before Christ or rather later is not certain – he came among the ancient peoples as a tall, fair-bearded man who was a great civilizer and law-giver, a priest-king of rare compassion and understanding. Both scientist and artist, he introduced the staple diet of maize and, like the Buddha, had a horror of violence towards living things. Subsequent practitioners of his wise and gentle religion took on the name Quetzalcoatl, a confusion that explains the blend of fact and myth surrounding the story of the Plumed Serpent.

Legend has it that as the boy-god grew up, evil magicians tried in vain to tempt him to perform human sacrifices. Chief among these tempters was the malevolent god Tezcatlipoca, who became the Aztec god of war and sacrifice,

Huitzilopochtli. One of his wicked ploys was to deck Quetzalcoatl in finery and to ply him with strong wine. This time he succumbed to temptation, and during a drunken debauch slept with his sister.

Later, when sober, Quetzalcoatl was stricken with horror at what he had done – and knew that penance would have to be paid. Accordingly he and his servants marched to the eastern seashore and there the Plumed Serpent dressed himself in his feathered robes and turquoise mask, built a funeral pyre and threw himself upon it. A flock of birds bore his ashes aloft and he ascended to the heavens as the planet Venus, where, until the date prophesied for his return, he watched over his lands and people. In this story of self-immolation lie the seeds of the later cults of wholesale human sacrifice, cults which Lawrence was to recapture in such stories as *The Woman Who Rode Away*.

Among the earliest of the great pre-Conquest cultures was that of the Mayans. They were based in the jungle city of Chichén Itzá in Yucatán to the east, and the 'City of the Gods', Teotihuacán, situated some 30 miles north-east of modern-day Mexico City. This is the site of the massive Pyramids to the Sun and the Moon, and the famous Temple of Quetzalcoatl, decorated with the sculptures of snarling serpents, that so impressed Lawrence when he went there in 1923.

A FLOURISHING CULTURE

Although human sacrifice was occasionally practised, the religion that dominated these societies still owed something to the gentle and wise ways of the original Quetzalcoatl. For 300 years there was a remarkable flourishing of the arts and sciences. Priests and scholars developed esoteric hieroglyphic scripts and a complex system of time and dates, based on the most precise astronomical calculations.

The Mayans fixed the length of a year (that is, one revolution of the earth round the sun) only a

Sacrificial victim
The Mayans believed that the world could be redeemed only by means of annual sacrifices. To that end Tezcatlipoca, god of all things of this world, donned the human skin of a sacrificial victim, as the Plumed Serpent (below), symbol of the green earth, opened his jaws to receive the body.

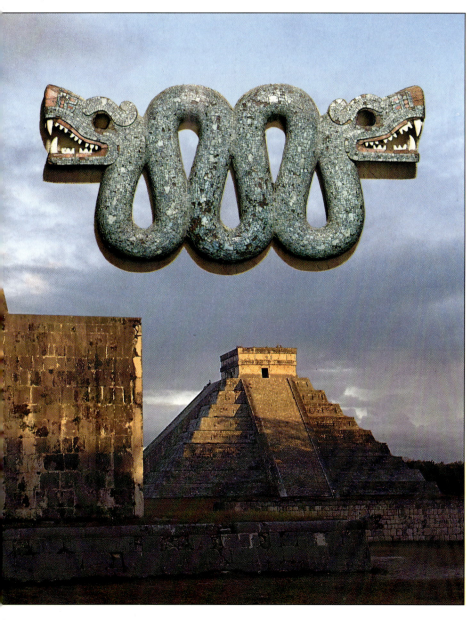

Tony Morrison/South American Pictures

Diego Rivera: The Totonac Civilisation (detail). INBA/National Palace, Mexico City/Giraudon

Concepts of time
In Mexican concepts of time, myth and science overlap. The huge calendar stone (left) is Aztec. Carved c. 1503, it represents the present in the centre, with earlier ages surrounding it. Although time was viewed cyclically rather than mathematically, their year was within seconds of our own.

few seconds short of modern calculations. The religious calendar, however, ran to only 260 days (in parts of Mexico and Guatemala the old system is still used and the days are called by their ancient names).

By a complicated calculation involving these two time-spans, a sacred period of 52 years was incorporated into the calendar, during which fires were lit to symbolize the continuation of time. At the end of each of these periods new fires were kindled to ensure that the world did not come to an end.

The ancients' concept of time is fundamental to an understanding of their civilization. In *Mornings in Mexico,* Lawrence says that for the Mexican Indian, "time is a vague, foggy reality", whereas to the Westerner, imagined by Lawrence as representing some form of "white monkey" to the Mexican, "The day is a horrible puzzle of exact spots of time".

The Mexicans' elastic view of time, which can exasperate the European visitor, is rooted very firmly in the old mythology. It is a cyclical rather than a chronological view of the passing of time, a system based on the revolution of the planets in which days, months and years each had their own gods – yesterday could quite easily become tomorrow because all time constantly recurred. This ideology exerted an extraordinary influence over individuals, and dictated, according to the time and day of their birth, their every action – even how and when they would die.

'MASTER CRAFTSMEN'
The so-called Classic period of ancient Mexico came to an abrupt end in about A.D. 900, probably as a result of epidemic, drought and invasion. A tribe called the Toltecs then took over power in the region of Teotihuacán.

Their name means 'Master Craftsmen', and the Toltecs produced some of the most beautiful artefacts of the pre-Hispanic era. Some say that one of their rulers, Topiltzin, was an incarnation of Quetzalcoatl. Certainly the Plumed Serpent was one of their chief deities, together with the wayward and powerful Tezcatlipoca, 'Lord of the Smoking Mirror', to whom they made human sacrifices.

On Tezcatlipoca's feast day, a youth chosen

Primitive rituals
As Lawrence wrote, "The Indian is completely embedded in the wonder of his own drama". Even today, Mexicans remain dazzled by their heritage. The 20th-century artist Diego Rivera often drew on this rich past for inspiration, as in the painting above.

for his presumed likeness to the god would regard it as an honour to give up his life. For twelve months before his sacrifice, he would be the object of great reverence, cherished and accorded the respect normally reserved for gods.

In the uncorrupted teachings and example of Quetzalcoatl, sacrifice had been an ideal only, a symbolic giving up of one's heart as a way to perfect love and understanding. In the Toltec culture, as in those that preceded it, the myth was acted out in real life.

When the heroine of Lawrence's short story *The Woman Who Rode Away* is asked by her Indian captors, "do you bring your heart to the god of Chilchui?", she automatically answers yes – meaning that she is willing to absorb herself in the mystery of their religion and culture. Only later does "An icy pang of fear and certainty" grip her heart as she realizes that their intention is to sacrifice her to their god.

The Aztecs who followed the Toltec culture in the Mexican Valley region, appropriating their deities and adding some of their own, compounded this misconception in the most barbarous way imaginable. In the space of a few hundred years the 'Heron People' – spurred on by their brutish war god Huitzilopochtli ('Left-handed Hummingbird'), who required a constant replenishment of fresh, bleeding hearts – rose from beggarly origins to reign supreme over much of Mexico.

Theirs was a militaristic society. The Aztecs tyrannized their empire, and so feared and hated did they become that at the time of the Spanish Conquest of Mexico in the 16th century, their subject peoples had no hesitation in siding with the Spanish.

Yet the Aztec civilization was one of considerable cultural achievement and interest. The city of

Alan Hutchison Library

Tony Morrison/South American Pictures

Quetzalcoatl
The head of the Plumed Serpent (above and left) juts out on either side of the steps of the temple dedicated to him at Teotihuacán. It dates from AD 700.

Tenochtitlán, built on a lake, was a triumph of engineering and architecture, which to the conquistadors (the conquering Spaniards) appeared as 'an enchanted vision'. Its people were musical and artistic and daily life centred on religious festivals. On their innumerable feast days the populace became divinely drunk on tequila, pulque and mescal, while the priests routinely took massive doses of hallucinatory drugs, derived from mushrooms and cacti, and fell into visionary states.

But the Aztecs' pre-eminence came to depend more and more on the perpetual waging of war – which kept neighbouring tribes in subjection and accrued great riches – and on ceaseless blood-letting to appease Huitzilopochtli. It was a case of a political imperative being justified and encouraged by religious orthodoxy, and it was taken to quite absurd lengths. The 'Xochiyaoyotl', or ritual 'War of the Flowers', was a contest to the death between Aztec warriors and those from subject tribes, which was designed to maintain a steady flow of sacrificial hearts even in 'peacetime'.

Mask of Tezcatlipoca
It was to the fearsome god Tezcatlipoca (left) that human sacrifices were made. On his particular feast day a youth, judged to be the earthly image of the god, was sacrificed in his honour. The boy apparently gave up his life willingly, believing that therein lay a higher form of existence.

Another bizarre rite was the fertility dance dedicated to the god of seed-time and planting, Xipe Totec, the 'Flayed One'. Prisoners from the latest fighting would be sacrificed and the priests would then peel off their skins in a single piece. While the skinless carcase was chopped up and taken away to be feasted on, the priests would don the skins like a body suit and lead a ritual dance from house to house.

HUMAN SACRIFICES

The most notorious of the Aztec rulers was Ahuitzotl, whose name has passed down into the language – 'Qué ahuitzote!', say Mexicans, meaning 'How fierce!' At the dedication ceremony of the Great Temple of Tenochtitlán he ordered the sacrifice of 20,000 prisoners captured in battle. They awaited their fate standing in four lines, more than three miles long.

The victims were spread-eagled over a saddle-shaped stone by four priests holding their arms and legs. The executioner would then stab the obsidian knife into their chests, rummage with his other hand, and wrench free the still-pumping hearts, which he then held aloft, proffering them to the sun. This slaughter at the Great Temple continued for four days until the city stank from the smell of human blood.

Such atrocities were committed in the name of a religion dominated by the mythological

Sacrificial knife
Below is the knife used to gouge out the hearts of the human sacrifices. The handle represents a crouching star god, poised to catch the blood of the victim.

'Saddle-shaped stone'
Although the precise function of the figure at right is in doubt, many believe that it was on this 'saddle-shaped stone' that sacrificial victims had their hearts ripped from their bodies. Pairs of priests would bind the victim's hands and head, and lay him face upwards on the stone, then one priest would plunge the sacrificial knife into his chest before raising the heart upwards in an offering to the sun.

figures of Huitzilopochtli and Quetzalcoatl, who represented the opposite forces of war and peace, darkness and light, evil and good.

It was this duality that appealed to Lawrence and found an echo in his own preoccupations with the reconciliation of opposing forces as a way to cosmic understanding. In *The Plumed Serpent* Cipriano "was Huitzilopochtli, Ramon was Quetzalcoatl", intent on purging a people that "took more satisfaction in ultimately destroying their heroes, than . . . raising them high".

THE PLUMED SERPENT'S REVENGE

The bloody Aztec civilization may have destroyed everything that Quetzalcoatl had originally stood for, but he was to have the last laugh. The conquistadors landed in the New World in the very year (1519) when, according to legend, Quetzalcoatl would return to his people and lands. It was a coincidence that struck terror into the hearts of the Aztecs, who believed that the great Plumed Serpent had come back to wreak vengeance on their degenerate culture. Demoralized and fearful, they proved no match for the Spanish leader, Hernán Cortés, and his small army. They easily captured Tenochtitlán (which was rebuilt as Mexico City), despite being overwhelmingly outnumbered, and the Aztec civilization was extinguished forever.

ROBERT GRAVES

✦ *1895 - 1985* ✦

Cordelia Weedon: Robert Graves

Robert Graves' life spanned nearly a century, a century in which he did "the usual storybook things" – he came to manhood, went to war, took life, loved unhappily, married, fathered children, wrote, gained recognition, found love and, essentially, lived happily ever after. Yet behind that list hides a man who only operated by his own rules, in his own time scale, according to his own personal and poetic mythology – a talented man of intense and uncompromising passions.

IN SEARCH OF A MUSE

Never quite at home in the twentieth century, Robert Graves pursued a life true to his poetic principles, searching for a Muse he could serve as man and poet.

The Graves family
Alfred Perceval Graves was a widower with five children when he married Amalie von Ranke. They had five more children: (left to right) Charles, Clarissa, Rosaleen, John and Robert.

Robert von Ranke Graves was a rare individual, an English bohemian of sorts who lived life according to his own rules, not society's. He shunned conventional jobs, social responsibilities (save during the war) and contemporary poetic movements. He was an uncompromising outsider, even as a child, and remained an elusive figure, shrouded in his own poetic myth throughout his life.

Graves was born in London on 24 July 1895, the third of five children. His father was an inspector of schools, the editor of an Irish literary magazine and a minor poet. However, despite these accomplishments he did not, according to Graves, try "to teach me how to write" or show "any understanding of my serious poetry." Nonetheless, the house was always full of books and the two were to share a lifelong passion for literature.

Graves' mother played a less significant role in shaping the future poet. She censored his reading, "believing that innocence was the surest protection against . . . dirtiness and intrigue and lustfulness", as Graves later wrote in his autobiography. Her strong puritan instinct instilled in him a fear of divine retribution which, allied with his own growing sexual fears, created a recurring sense of terror. As an adult, Graves frequently wrestled with this demon, trying to reconcile it with his own innately loving nature.

Unhappy schooldays
"From the moment I arrived at the school [Charterhouse] I suffered an oppression of spirit that I hesitate now to recall in its full intensity . . . My clothes were all wrong . . . My name appeared on the school list as 'R. von R. Graves' . . . 'German' meant 'dirty German' . . . and the legend was put about that I was not only a German but a German-Jew . . . My last resource was to sham insanity . . . It succeeded unexpectedly well. Soon nobody troubled me."

ers, he was soon posted to the front line. The hell of no-man's-land, bedecked with a "frozen parade" of corpses, forced him to the conclusion that the only certain means of staying alive involved getting wounded and being sent back home to England. Although he did not actively seek injury, that is precisely what happened to him in July 1916.

Graves was seriously wounded and badly shocked by an explosion, with pieces of shell lodged deep within his chest and thigh. But the army mistakenly informed his parents that 'your son has died of wounds. He was very gallant . . . and is a great loss', later even forwarding them his personal belongings. It was left to Graves to sort out the confusion, which meant requesting *The Times* to announce that his recently printed obituary had been highly premature!

While recuperating in England, Graves became a good friend of the war poet Siegfried Sassoon. Both were so outraged at the mismanagement and

Graves' early schooling was not particularly happy because he was usually regarded as something of an oddity. As a young child, he went to no less than six schools, sometimes for as little as a term; because of his own unhappiness or because of his father's dissatisfaction with the standard of teaching at each place, he was continually moved on. When he was 13, he went to Charterhouse public (private) school which rapidly became, as it had for William Thackeray 70 years before, a psychological 'slaughterhouse'. Even half a century after leaving there, Graves still had nightmares about his wretched experiences. His major problems arose from his abiding love of literature which nobody seemed to understand or to share; from the fact that his name appeared on the school list as 'R. von R. Graves', which his peers seized on as proof of his German allegiance at a time when anti-German prejudice ran high; and from his parents' reluctance to buy him a smart school uniform in an environment noted for its total and unquestioning privilege.

SHAMMING INSANITY

The consequence of his unremitting victimization was that he started to have problems with his heart and nearly suffered a breakdown, after which he decided to "sham insanity", wearing straws in his hair, to ensure that he was left alone. "It succeeded unexpectedly well", he later wrote. Gradually, though, he eased himself out of this role, taking up boxing and developing several strong friendships which made his final school years somewhat more bearable.

When Graves was 19, he put off the opportunity to study English at Oxford, fearing an arid, unimaginative approach to the subject he felt so deeply about. Instead, he enlisted in the army believing, as did so many others, that the war which had just started would soon be over.

Although Graves' army career began slowly, filled with tedious spells guarding German prison-

Harlech countryside
The cool 'indifference' of the terrain around their home in North Wales (above) appealed to Graves: "Once, when I came home on leave from the war (right) I spent about a week of my ten days walking about on these hills to restore my sanity."

Key Dates

1895 born in London
1916 wounded; poems published
1918 marries Nancy Nicholson
1919 moves to Boar's Hill, Oxford
1926 meets Laura Riding
1929 *Goodbye to All That;* settles in Mallorca
1934 *I, Claudius*
1940–46 Vale House Farm, Devon
1946 returns to Deyá, Mallorca
1948 *The White Goddess*
1950 marries Beryl Hodge
1955 *The Greek Myths*
1961–66 Professor of Poetry at Oxford
1985 dies in Deyá

calamitous reality of the war that they considered making a formal protest. Sassoon in fact did so, but Graves, anxious for his welfare, persuaded him to be examined by a medical board, who pronounced him shell-shocked and in need of hospital treatment.

When Graves had barely recovered from his physical injuries, he returned to the battlefield in France, where, despite a severe attack of bronchitis and periods of shell shock, he walked up to 12 miles a day through the deep, sucking mud, to and from the front line. Eventually, though, the doctors pronounced him unfit for duty and, in 1917, threatened him with a court martial if he did not return home.

The following year, Graves fell in love with the robust, unconventional Nancy Nicholson, whom he married a year later. Soon after, they had

E T Archive

Wartime marriage
Not long after their marriage in 1918, Robert and Nancy (above) moved to Boar's Hill near Oxford where, for £3 a month, they rented a cottage from the poet John Masefield. With high expectations, Nancy set up a traditional village shop there (right), where you could 'buy everything from a collar-stud to a saucepan'. However, notwithstanding her willingness 'to execute an order for any article not in stock', the shop was a financial disaster.

Miss Nicholson ready to execute an order for any article not in stock. The business is most go-ahead, and no effort is spared to give satisfaction.

The Hon. Mrs. Michael Howard (left) with Miss Nancy Nicholson outside the shop.

Two little customers arrive. Every want is supplied from stock or to order.

The Hon. Mrs. Michael Howard and Miss Nicholson, sister of the famous artist, have opened an "all sorts" shop at Boar's Hill, Oxfordshire, a colony which includes such well-known poets as the Poet Laureate (Dr. Bridges), Mr. John Masefield and others. The sign was painted by Mr. Nicholson.—(*Daily Mirror* photographs.)

British Library

their first child and then moved to the rural out-skirts of Oxford, as Graves had now decided to commence his university studies. However, this was a fairly unsatisfactory period for him because the marriage started to founder. At first he hoped to be able to renew their love, writing Nancy a poem: "Give then a thought for me/Walking so miserably . . . Swallow your pride, let us be as we used to be." But Nancy regretted their marriage and, as Graves wrote in 1929, wanted "somehow to be dis-married". She did not, however, want to leave him, and over the next three years they had three more children.

Egyptian interlude
In 1926 Graves, Nancy, their children and the newly-arrived Laura Riding sailed to Cairo, where Graves was to be Professor of English. Within a few months, however, they abandoned the venture and returned to England, disenchanted with a 'land where the dead parade the streets'.

H. S. D. Corrodi: An Egyptian Bazaar/Christie's

H. Corrodi Roma

Siegfried Sassoon
Dubbed 'Mad Jack' for his recklessness, Siegfried Sassoon met Graves in the trenches of Northern France – two soldier-poets of the Royal Welch Fusiliers. Amid hammering rain, an abundance of rats and the constant sound of shelling, they read each other's poems and formed a powerful friendship. But later they quarrelled bitterly.

National Portrait Gallery, London

Meanwhile, Graves completed his studies and began his lifelong devotion to his Muse, writing eight volumes of poetry between 1920 and 1925. As he later wrote: "Since the age of fifteen poetry has been my ruling passion and I have never intentionally undertaken any task or formed any relationship that seemed inconsistent with poetic principles; which has sometimes won me the reputation of an eccentric." But living out his 'poetic' life was not quite so easy. Graves' problem now, as at various points throughout his life, was to find a woman who could be the human embodiment of his Muse, and whom he could serve as both a man and a poet.

FINDING A GODDESS

Graves could not cast Nancy in this role since she was wholly unlike a Muse, being radical in many of her views and outspoken in her "universal condemnation of men". However, after a difficult period of fruitless searching, he found a woman who did become his incarnate Goddess. In 1926, after a lengthy transatlantic correspondence, Graves finally met the 25-year-old American poet, Laura Riding. He had been offered a teaching post in Cairo and, perennially short of funds, had accepted. Exactly one week after meeting Laura Riding, he set sail with her, his wife Nancy, their four children and a nanny, for Egypt. Laura quickly became the dominant, though not always beneficial force in his life. Initially, their relationship was cemented by their mutal belief in the sanctity of poetry, but gradually their meeting of minds became also a meeting of bodies. Cairo proved less than enthralling, however, and within six months the bizarre 'family' were back on English shores.

Nancy did not seem to object to Graves and Laura's liaison and even attempted to quieten the mounting gossip. By now though, it was evident to all their friends that Graves had found his inspiration. Graves was revitalized by Laura's lively, sympathetic interest in him and what was the most important part of him – his poetry.

Not long after, Graves began living with Laura,

falling ever more completely under her influence. She even managed to convince him that she had total control over time and change, and eventually got him to agree to the ludicrous proposition that 'bodies have had their day' when, in 1933, she insisted they became celibate.

One of the main reasons Graves never questioned Laura's role as a 'superior' being, willingly submitting his work to her for approval and subsidising her various literary and non-literary projects, was because, as his Muse, she was both an inspiration and a demanding task master. In short, she appealed to his highly developed sense of Romantic masochism.

However, this 'Holy Trinity', as Graves, his mistress and his wife became known, soon became the 'Four'. This happened in 1929, when the Irishman Geoffrey Phibbs began a literary collaboration with Laura, who gradually fell hopelessly in love with him. Yet this intricate, potentially highly damaging, emotional tangle involving four very different people eventually became too much for Phibbs; he fled from their London home and escaped briefly to France and his abandoned wife Norah. Forced back by the 'Trinity', and in particular by the desperate Laura, he surprised everyone by announcing that from then on he

LAURA RIDING

From 1926 to 1939 Robert Graves had an increasingly demanding and uneasy relationship with the American poet Laura Riding. Born in New York in 1901, she became involved with a group of writers known as the Fugitives before she left America because of their lack of 'complete poetic seriousness'. Graves had the seriousness she was searching for and together they wrote and collaborated on a number of books until, for Laura, more stimulating mentors entered the scene. With the passage of time Riding went from being Graves' Muse to his 'Queen Famine'.

Kenneth Gay

wanted to live with Graves' wife Nancy, not with Laura.

Laura was so devastated by this revelation that she immediately tried to commit suicide. She took a drink of disinfectant and leapt from a fourth-floor window, whereupon Graves dashed down one flight of stairs, and then threw himself out of a third-floor window. Somehow, he survived the fall, and was able to help the badly injured Laura into an ambulance.

As things calmed down over the following weeks, the 'Four' sorted themselves out. The extraordinary incident culminated with Phibbs going to live with Nancy and her children, as he had intended, while Graves and Laura resumed their eccentric partnership.

While Laura was recovering from her fall, Graves wrote the first of his bestsellers, written for no other reason than to make money. Yet though Graves usually, and Laura always, dismissed them as potboilers (because they were written in prose, not poetry), they were in fact, almost without exception, fine works of art. *Goodbye to All That* was the first of these pieces, a brilliant autobiography tackling Graves' experiences at school and in the trenches, and the break-up of his marriage.

MALLORCAN EXILE

With the profits from this book Graves and Laura left England – and the gossip surrounding her suicide bid – for Mallorca. It was this Spanish island which, save for one period of enforced exile, became his home for the rest of his life. Unfortunately life there soon hit problems because their money began to run out, and their relationship was strained by Laura's uncompromising demands. They concentrated on their writing, separately and together, and ran a printing press (an enterprise they had started in England) on which they printed limited editions of their works.

Graves' poems, however, never made him any money. So, in order to build up his dwindling finances, he set about another prose work which he was determined would be a bestseller. In fact *I, Claudius*, published in 1934, turned out to be a greater financial and literary success than he could have imagined, both enabling him to pay for a new house and establishing his reputation as one of the finest writers of the time.

Sadly, Graves' spell of good fortune was temporarily interrupted by the fascist takeover of Mallorca, forcing him and Laura to seek refuge elsewhere from 1936. But though over the next few years they lived in England, Switzerland and America, the turbulence of his everyday life never affected the quality or stability of his writing.

There are few obvious divides in Graves' life, but without doubt one of them occurred in 1939. Laura fell in love with Schuyler Jackson, a married American, who soon assumed Graves' role as her intellectual and loving companion. Fortunately Graves was spared a lengthy period of unhappiness because he too now met a new partner. His

'Mid-Winter Waking'
After his self-destructive relationship with Laura Riding, growing to know and to love the gentle Beryl Hodge was an extraordinary process of awakening. In a poem inspired by her and aptly titled 'Mid-Winter Waking', he wrote, "Stirring suddenly from long hibernation,/I knew myself once more a poet/ . . . And presently dared open both my eyes." From 1940 to 1946 they lived in a farmhouse (below) in the small village of Galmpton in Devon.

relationship with the serene Beryl Hodge provided him with the domestic tranquillity that he had so lacked with Laura.

Graves celebrated their union with many tender verses –

"*You of your gentleness,
I of my rashness,
Both of despair –
Yet still might share
This happy will.*"

In another poem he likens his love for Beryl to that of "knowing myself once more a poet". And he did indeed write some of his finest poetry between 1938 and 1945. Meanwhile the atmosphere of his home life radically improved, too, as friends, who had been driven away by the daunting presence of Laura, began to return, and Graves' house filled with the bubbling noises of three children born between 1940 and 1944.

The year 1944 was also momentous for Graves because it was when he began his major poetic

Douglas Glass © J. C. Glass

Shared pleasures
Graves and his second family enjoy the Mallorcan sunshine and the relaxed spirit of the island. With Beryl, Graves had four children: William (1940), Lucia (1943), Juan (1944) and Tomas, not shown (1953).

BBC Hulton Picture Library

Home sweet home
When Graves was finally able to return to his treasured house, called Canelluñ (below), in Deyá, Mallorca, he was delighted to find everything just as he had left it before the war. As he wrote to his friend and fellow-writer Alan Hodge (Beryl's first husband), 'everything was ten years older but just the same: for example, all my shirts and trousers and socks wearable; and five jars of green tomato chutney, eatable; and cigarette tobacco in my tobacco jar, smokeable.'

statement, *The White Goddess*, shortly after which he returned from his European exile to Mallorca, this time with Beryl. However, while he continued writing poems, essays and prose, one vital element was holding him back: he lacked an incarnate Muse. Beryl never qualified for this role – in fact, had she done so, a long, happy relationship with her might have become impossible – and she does not appear to have objected when, from 1950 to 1952, Graves became very close to yet another woman whom he regarded as his inspiration. Then followed a lean six-year spell as a creative writer – when ironically his fame as a distinguished poet spread to America – until he met his next inspirational Muse.

RULED BY POETRY
Although Graves revered the women whom he cast as his Muses, he was never tempted to leave Beryl for them, though at times she must have felt deeply wounded by his attachments. Further-

'Adopted son'
A small fishing village of some 450 inhabitants, Deyá (left) was Graves' spiritual home from 1929. Forty years later the inhabitants paid him an honour which to him matched any literary prize he received in his lifetime: they made him an 'adopted son' of the village – the first and only one ever in the history of Deyá.

Douglas Glass © J. C. C. Glass

Fact or Fiction

I, ROBERT GRAVES . . .

Although *I, Claudius'* hero is clearly the Roman Emperor Claudius I (ruled AD 41-54), there are aspects of his character which are strikingly similar to Graves' view of himself. For example, Graves always saw himself as an outsider, and, like Claudius, he often cultivated that role. While Graves was without stutter or physical deformity, he nevertheless felt himself somehow defective. Long after *I, Claudius* was published, Graves wrote a poem entitled *The Second-Fated* in which he and Claudius merge more pointedly: in it Graves opens with the words "My stutter, my cough, my unfinished sentences . . ."

Louvre, Paris/Giraudon

more, despite his growing fame he chose never to abandon his spartan lifestyle. He remained "nobody's servant [having] chosen to live on the outskirts of a Majorcan mountain village . . . where life is still ruled by the old agricultural cycle." And poetry remained his "ruling passion".

Yet lack of money forced him to accept several offers to write filmscripts and give lectures, not all of which were disagreeable to him. He also wrote *The Greek Myths*, in which he "connected a lot of mythical patterns which were not connected before". In his mid-sixties, as one of the great writers of his generation, he was offered the CBE (which he declined, not believing in the honours' system), and in 1961 he became Professor of Poetry at Oxford, one of the most popular ever holders of this prestigious post.

Graves kept up his stream of writing until he was 75, and from then on lived quietly in his adopted Mallorcan village of Deyá. He died peacefully, aged 90, on 7 December 1985, among his loved ones and his cherished surroundings. As he would have wished, his gravestone reads simply 'Robert Graves, Poeta'.

William Graves

I, CLAUDIUS

Densely packed with people, action and intrigue, Claudius' account of life in and around the palace is a chilling view of brutality and greed.

One of the most ambitious historical novels attempted this century, *I, Claudius* is presented as an autobiography and depicts all the intrigue, immorality and brutality characteristic of the Roman Empire. The self-effacing Claudius conceals nothing in his attempt to record the bloody reigns of Augustus, Tiberius and Caligula for posterity. The result is a fascinating, at times blood-curdling, account of the minds and motives behind the political structure of the Roman Empire for half a century from 10BC. With extraordinary dexterity, Robert Graves brings ancient history to life by having us listen directly to Claudius – a man of such humility and integrity that we cannot fail to trust his word and be moved by him.

"Claudius the Idiot" or "Claudius the Stammerer", as he is known by friends and relatives, decides to write the "strange history of my life" after consulting the Sybil Amalthea. Her utterance in Greek

At the Senate
(right) Augustus' "influence on the Senate was such that they voted whatever he suggested to them." He tries as best he can to restore "Rome to peace and security after the long disasters of the Civil Wars".

Consummate ambition
(below) "Livia was unique in setting no limit at all" to her ambitions. With an impressive host of informers, she quells all hints of insurrection before they start.

Sir L. Alma-Tadema: An Audience. Dick Institue, Kilmarnock/Bridgeman Art Library

W. H. Barraud: News from Afar/Fine Art Photographic Library

verse ends with the prophetic lines:
"But when he's dumb and no more here,
Nineteen hundred years or near.
Clau-Clau-Claudius shall speak clear."

GUIDE TO THE PLOT

Believing it to be his duty to record an honest account of his life, Claudius begins his story with his grandmother Livia, "one of the worst of the Claudians". It is her ambition to gain power by returning Republican Rome to a monarchy. Recognizing Augustus as a surer bet for king than her own husband, she divorces Claudius' grandfather and marries Augustus, binding him to her with "shame and unslakable passion". Their marriage is never consummated, however, giving Livia a lifelong hold over Augustus.

While Livia engineers and schemes both within the palace and in affairs of state, Augustus sets about restoring Rome to peace and security after the lengthy civil wars. The Senate, recognizing his increasing power, votes to designate him a god, making him king in all but name. Meanwhile Livia continues to plot and plan for the future, ensuring that her branch of the family are in line for the monarchy. Anyone in her way is banished on some

First love
(above) "Nearly every day" Claudius and the beautiful Medullina meet secretly in the garden to talk and read together – and, occasionally, kiss.

> "That man ought to be put out of the way! He's as stupid as a donkey – what am I saying? Donkeys are sensible beings by comparison – he's as stupid as…as…Heavens, he's as stupid as my son Claudius!"

A prophecy
(right) Visiting the Sibyl at Cumae, Claudius learns to his astonishment that his destiny and Rome's are fatefully and irrevocably intertwined.

trumped-up charge or mysteriously dies.

Our unlikely hero, Claudius, is born premature and sickly, growing up with a nervous tic, a stammer and a permanent limp. An affectionate and clever child, he is treated with cruelty and contempt by all his family except his brother Germanicus and cousin Postumus. Thanks to the kind attentions of his tutor Athenodorus, he develops a love for history, spending long periods reading and writing.

Claudius' uncle Tiberius, of "suspicious, jealous, reserved and melancholy temperament", is worked hard by Augustus and begs his mother Livia to release him from his duties and from his failed marriage with Julia, Augustus' beloved daughter. He retires to Rhodes, away from the political machinations of Rome, and waits for Livia's summons to come and take power when the time is right. Poor Julia, fed a drug by Livia which "so

stimulated her sexual appetite that she became like a demented woman", is finally banished to a tiny desolate island as punishment for her infidelities.

With Julia and Tiberius out of the way, Livia next manages to remove Postumus, Julia's only true-hearted son, from the centre of power by fabricating charges of rape against him. Unjustly expelled, he is later freed from his island prison by Augustus, but does not survive long enough to seriously threaten Livia and Tiberius' rule. His death leaves the monarchy open for Tiberius, who begins his period of office with moderation. He knows he has to thank Livia for his position; they have "an understanding between them of guarded co-operation".

The long struggles with occupied but restless countries leave the Roman armies short of fighting men. Bad terms and conditions of service lead to a series of mutinies which only Germanicus, Claudius' elder brother, is able to control. The opposite of Tiberius in every respect, Germanicus is a huge favourite with the Roman people. Clearly fearful of Germanicus' popularity, Tiberius sets about making life extremely difficult for him.

The rise of Sejanus, an evil-minded go-

In the Background

VESTAL VIRGINS

The Vestal Virgins were priestesses of Vesta, goddess of the hearth, and their duty was to keep a sacred fire going in her temple at all times. Chosen from noble families, they started young – between the ages of six and ten – and undertook to serve for at least 30 years. If they broke their vow of chastity during their term of office, they were buried alive.

between for Tiberius and his elaborate network of informers, brings wholesale corruption to the Roman system of government. Tiberius' mounting greed and depravity make him suspicious of everyone, and lead him to choose Caligula as a successor – a man more base and corrupt than even Tiberius himself.

Aware of his vulnerability, Claudius tries to maintain a low profile, relying on his physical handicaps to keep him out of danger. Against his will, he is married several times – first to Urgulanilla, the monstrously ugly daughter of Livia's spy and confidante, and second to Sejanus' adopted sister Aelia. His happiest domestic times are with the prostitute Actë, whom he keeps in his villa out of town, and her successor Calpurnia, who turns out to be his most trusted friend.

Not even Claudius can escape the inevitability of fate, however, and eventually, as an ageing man, he is forced back to the Palace to take his allotted place in the scheme of things.

INTRIGUE AND TREACHERY

I, Claudius is a fast moving and densely packed account of life among the nobility in Rome when the Empire was reaching its peak. Claudius knows that he is writing only about the core of government and the few hundred or so people affected by its rottenness. The vivid descriptions of battles, sword-fighting in the amphitheatres, palace life, the Senate at work, all serve to enrich the essential story of how power is maintained and passed on from one emperor to another.

The brilliant device of giving the role of narrator to Claudius means the story comes alive, reading almost as an eye-witness account of events. Being an outcast of the noble family and therefore detached from the main thrust of political intrigue, and being driven by a historian's quest for truth, Claudius becomes the perfect biographer. It is not just his own life story he is relating, but those of all his family from Augustus onwards. Claudius says he writes without restraint, with the "hope that you, my eventual readers of a hundred generations ahead or more, will feel yourselves directly spoken to, as if by a contemporary".

Claudius' grandfather, believing that Augustus will restore "the ancient liberties of the people", supports him in his battles for power against Pompey and Antony. But he reckoned without Livia: "Augustus ruled the world, but Livia ruled Augustus." Her relentless drive to consolidate her own power means Rome moves further and further away from

being a republic. Her hatred for the common people is fierce: "Rabble and slaves! The Republic was always a humbug. What Rome really needs is a king again."

Between them, Livia and Augustus tirelessly impose a series of legal, social, administrative, religious and military reforms which, on the surface, all appear to be in the best interests of the State. But any opposition is removed by military defeat, secret murder or public execution. Claudius observes, "Had their sole and arbitrary power not been disguised under the forms of ancient liberty they would never have held it long."

H. Siemiradzki: At the Well/Christie's

Loyal mistress
(above) Living with Claudius in his villa outside Rome, the prostitute Calpurnia counsels him wisely. He is happier with her than with any of his four 'noble' wives.

> "I could never have thought it possible that I would miss Livia when she died. When I was a child I used secretly, night after night, to pray to the Infernal Gods to carry her off. And now I would have offered the richest sacrifices I could find – unblemished white bulls and desert antelopes and ibises and flamingoes by the dozen – to have had her back again."

Fatal attractions
Caligula's acts of madness extend to the women he 'loved' – even, Claudius suspects, to his favourite sister Drusilla, who dies mysteriously. "Whenever he kissed a woman now, I am told, he used to say: 'As white and lovely a neck as this is, I have only to give the word, and slash! it will be cut clean through.'"

Georges-Antoine Rochegrosse: Roman Justice, 1916/©DACS 1989/Fine Art Photographic Library

Augustus, tired of state business and perpetual honours, longs to retire and let the State govern itself. But Livia, for whom supreme power "had come to be more important than life or honour", convinces him civil war will return and their lives be endangered if he becomes a mere private citizen again. Her judgement is accurate. With their unscrupulous elimination of all obstacles, they have created a host of enemies. And so, having amassed power, Livia's most urgent task is to maintain it. All the 'good' Claudians – Drusus, Agrippina, Germanicus, and Postumus – threaten her absolute power by their belief in the Republic. She explains to Claudius towards the end of her life why their ideal is absurd: "You refuse

to see that one can no more reintroduce republican government at this stage than one can reimpose primitive feelings of chastity on modern wives and husbands. It's like trying to turn the shadow back on a sundial: it can't be done."

Livia's spies are everywhere and she keeps secret dossiers on anyone she suspects of treason. She knows the only way she can stay powerful after Augustus' death is by ensuring a weak and corrupt successor to the monarchy. Tiberius is certainly unscrupulous enough for the task, but deeply resents his mother's influence over his rule. His mounting greed and fear of assassination lead him to extreme acts of despotism. Confiscating the estates of rich nobles and summarily

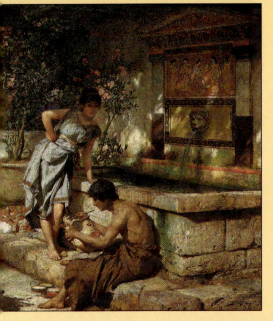

executing anyone on flimsy charges of treason, he rules Rome from the island of Capri, where he feels safer and can freely indulge his sexual excesses.

Fear governs the Senate: "The informers were still busy and every year more and more people were executed. There was hardly a senator left who had kept his seat since the days of Augustus." Gallus, the only outspoken critic of Tiberius' reign, is thrown to rot underground in a palace cell. Old Arruntius, the last link with the Augustan age, commits suicide, predicting that "Caligula with his Capri education will make a worse

Emperor even than Tiberius." As Livia has foreseen, Augustus' and Tiberius' vanity does not allow them to endure a successor who might be more popular than themselves. Tiberius therefore appoints the "treacherous, cowardly, lustful, vain, deceitful" Caligula and so the whole system perpetuates itself, becoming ever more tyrannical and perverted.

PROPHECY

There is a sense of inevitability about the dreadful bloodshed and brutality practised by the monarchy and their advisors during this period of Roman history. Claudius describes atrocity after atrocity in matter-of-fact tones, burying his sense of outrage in the face of such overwhelming odds. For not only do the emperors wield absolute power against which any resistance leads to certain death, but also the prophecies came true and therefore confirm the inescapability of fate.

The 'Punic Curse', referred to by the Sybil in Chapter 1, sets the scene. After utterly destroying Carthage in the Third Punic War, Rome has been "choked by a money madness", and with riches come "sloth, greed, cruelty, dishonesty, cowardice, effeminacy, and every other un-Roman vice." Honesty is punished, depravity rewarded.

Augustus, Livia and Tiberius set great store by prophecy. Tiberius expels all astrologers, magicians, and fortune-tellers from Rome to conceal his dependency on Thrasyllus, whom he regularly consults. Livia also sees Thrasyllus, whose predictions, she says, are never wrong. It is not enough for Livia to be powerful in her own lifetime: all her scheming will be wasted unless she knows what follows.

Claudius is haunted by prophetic hints concerning his future, the implications of which he manages to ignore for a long time. Aged eight, he catches a wolf cub in his gown that has been dropped by eagles flying overhead. His sister Livilla shrieks with disbelief when she overhears an elderly nobleman's interpretation of the event – "wretched Rome, with *him* as her protector!" Then later Briseis, an old servant of his mother's, tells Claudius of a dream she has one night. The warning that he should stay away from the palace until it is safe, is clear: "So choose a good tree, Master Claudius, and don't come down till the last of the thieves are dead."

This powerful sense of fate being in the hands of the gods makes Claudius' story all the more dramatic and compelling, especially as Claudius himself refuses to see how the future of Rome is also his own future.

Sir L. Alma-Tadema: A Bear Fight in the Coliseum/Fine Art Photographic Library

Costly excesses
(above) "What with buying all those animals and paying the huntsmen in the amphitheatres", Caligula squanders 7 million gold pieces in just three months.

Begging for mercy
When the soldiers riot, Claudius (right) fears for his life – but his fate is quite other than death.

Sir L. Alma-Tadema: Proclaiming Claudius Emperor. Forbes Magazine Collection, New York/Bridgeman Art Library

CHARACTERS IN FOCUS

The main characters in *I, Claudius* are memorable for their extremes of behaviour. According to Claudius, good Claudians are honourable, virtuous and loyal to the State, and bad Claudians are greedy, wicked and treacherous. But driven by ambition, fear, and other basic human emotions, the central characters are altogether more complex than Claudius would have us believe – and capable of extremes of cruelty made more brutal by their apparent casualness.

WHO'S WHO

Claudius The narrator, he is Livia's ill-favoured grandson.

Livia Third wife of Augustus, she is ruthlessly ambitious and rules her household, and Rome, with an iron will.

Augustus Compassionate and principled, his main fault as Emperor is that he is too heavily influenced by Livia.

Tiberius Livia's son by her first marriage, he is never popular and accedes to the throne only with his mother's aid.

Germanicus Claudius' beloved elder brother whose popularity makes him Augustus' obvious successor.

Calpurnia Claudius' caring and attentive mistress.

Julia "A decent, good-hearted woman", Augustus' adored daughter falls victim to Livia's scheming.

Postumus One of Augustus' most – and Livia's least – favourite grandsons, he is brave, outspoken and a true friend to Claudius.

Urgulania Livia's right hand in all her treachery and intrigue.

Sejanus Unscrupulous and evil-minded, he is Tiberius' envoy to the Senate.

Caligula Claudius' nephew; with his unbelievable vanity and capricious acts of sadism, he becomes the most hated ruler of all.

Ridiculed and rejected by his family, Claudius (above) goes through life with a stutter and a limp. But in spite of the widespread "physical repugnance" evoked by this "poor deaf, stammering cripple", "Claudius the Idiot" is far from stupid. Loyal to his friends, to Rome and to the truth, he survives the politics of power, rising from being "a wretched little oddity, a disgrace to so strong and magnificent a father and so fine and stately a mother" to being a Consul and, ultimately, Emperor of Rome.

"Calpurnia [right], a prostitute and the daughter of a prostitute, was more intelligent and loyal and kindhearted and straightforward than any of the four noblewomen I have married", Claudius tells us. His consort in his villa outside Rome, she is privy to his confidences and she counsels him wisely. She warns him of Caligula's excesses and accurately foresees the dangers to come; and later, when Claudius is depressed at being the constant butt of practical jokes, she reassures him: "you're luckier than you realize . . . people don't kill their butts" – at least he will be safe.

"One of the worst of the Claudians", Livia (left) is the omnipotent, malevolent power behind the throne. If anyone displeases her, or appears to threaten her or Augustus' Imperial supremacy, they suddenly and mysteriously disappear. No-one is safe – even her former husband and her son fall victim to her lust for power. "The name 'Livia' is connected with the Latin word which means Malignity", Claudius explains. "My grandmother was a consummate actress, and the outward purity of her conduct, the sharpness of her wit, and the graciousness of her manners deceived nearly everybody." Banishment and murder are among her weapons.

"A fine-looking man himself, though somewhat short", Augustus (above) had "curly fair hair that went grey only very late in his life". He is well-intentioned and a man of principle, but his better judgement is clouded by his wife Livia: "Augustus ruled the world, but Livia ruled Augustus." Although passionately devoted to her, "the truth is that the marriage was never consummated. Augustus, though capable enough with other women, found himself as impotent as a child when he tried to have commerce with my grandmother".

As a small boy Caligula (left) sets fire to Claudius' house in a "fit of temper", furious because Antonia, Claudius' mother, has dared to spank him. The house is razed to the ground. A few years later Antonia catches the 12-year-old Caligula and his 13-year-old sister Drusilla in an act of incest. "Caligula's a monster and Drusilla's a she-monster", Antonia hisses at her son. Aged 25 years, Caligula, proud of his barbarism, boasts to Claudius: "by the age of eight I had killed my father. Jove himself never did that . . . Not only did I kill my natural father but I killed my father by adoption too – Tiberius, you know. And whereas Jupiter only lay with one sister of his, Juno, I have lain with all three of mine."

OLYMPIAN DREAMER

Graves earned his living as a prose writer, but he regarded poetry as his life's mission, applying himself to it with a devotion that was almost religious in its intensity.

Robert Graves insisted again and again that "My only real work is now, and has always been, poems"; and it is as a poet, more than as a novelist, that he is likely to be remembered. During his lifetime, Graves' reputation fluctuated considerably. He first became known when his early poems appeared in Edward Marsh's *Georgian Poetry 1916-17*, but his lifelong refusal to follow fashions left his work largely neglected for years. Where other poets wrote lengthy 'ambitious' works, Graves generally confined himself to brief, intense, immaculately crafted verses that embodied his own ambivalent, idiosyncratic view of the relationship between man and woman. Only after World War II did his true stature gradually become apparent.

Private publishing

In 1928 Graves and his lover Laura Riding established the Seizin Press in London to publish small editions of books 'of a certain quality'. They used a magnificent Victorian hand press and laboured hard at mastering the technicalities of printing. The Press was later transferred to their home in Mallorca.

AN ACQUAINTANCE WITH DESCRIPTION

BY

GERTRUDE STEIN

Printed and published at The Seizin Press
35a St. Peter's Square Hammersmith
London 1929

TREASURE BOX
—

BY

ROBERT GRAVES

A PRIVATE PURSUIT

None of this worried Graves too much, since he regarded poetry as an essentially private pursuit and never expected to make money from it. He followed his own path with an almost fanatical integrity, inspired by his vision of the true poet as one who "treats poetry with a single-minded devotion which may be called religious, and . . . allows no other activity in which he takes part, whether concerned with his livelihood or with his social duties, to interfere with it. This has been my own rule since I was fourteen or fifteen, and has become second nature to me." Graves described this as 'muse poetry', as opposed to the verse of premeditated public statement, written in the hope of winning fame, which he condemned: "Poems should not be written, like novels, to entertain or instruct the public; or the less poems they." Hence his decision to omit his war poems from the various editions of his *Collected Poems*, on the grounds that they were really "higher journalism . . . too obviously written in the post-war poetry boom".

For Graves, there is only one authentic process of poetic composition. "A poet finds himself caught in some baffling emotional problem, which is of such

Wartime memories
(left) Graves was haunted by the death and destruction he witnessed in World War I, vividly recalling his experiences in his autobiography.

A famous friend
Graves enjoyed a close friendship with T. E. Lawrence, the celebrated Lawrence of Arabia (right), and wrote his biography in 1927. They had met in Oxford in 1919, and Graves considered him 'a great man on poetry, pictures, music and everything else in the world'.

H. S. Williamson: German Attack on a Wet Morning. Trustees of the Imperial War Museum

National Portrait Gallery, London

The White Goddess led Graves on to even more controversial investigations in, for example, *King Jesus* and *The Nazarene Gospel Restored* (1953).

He felt impelled to write these books; but most of Graves' prose works – unlike his poetry – were, he asserted, "written with a direct money-making purpose". In this he was remarkably successful, following up his popular book on his friend Lawrence of Arabia (*Lawrence and the Arabs*, 1927) with *Goodbye to All That* (1929), which Graves described as "a reckless autobiography . . . with small consideration for anyone's feelings". Its commercial success was in fact an accident of timing, since it appeared just when *All Quiet on the Western Front* and similarly unromantic books about World War I were coming into vogue; but its out-

urgency that it sends him into a sort of trance. And in this trance his mind works, with astonishing boldness and precision, on several imaginative levels at once. The poem is either a practical answer to his problem, or else it is a clear statement of it; and a problem clearly stated is half-way to solution." But when he comes out of the trance – or, as Graves called it elsewhere, self-hypnosis "as practised by the witch doctors, his ancestors in poetry" – the poet allows his conscious mind to start functioning and work over the material supplied by the Muse, since "every poem must make prose sense as well as poetic sense on one or more levels". Graves was himself a tireless reviser, on occasion producing more than thirty drafts of a single poem.

ERUDITION AND INGENUITY
Some of Graves' best known prose works were offshoots of his poetic commitment. Apart from his essays on poetry – often entertainingly vicious about all fellow-practitioners he disliked, from Milton to D. H. Lawrence – he published a fascinating mixture of anthropology, detection and guesswork in *The White Goddess*. This linked Gravesian poetic practice with the supposed existence of a universal Muse/Moon Goddess who reigned before her place was usurped by male deities, a thesis expounded by Graves with remarkable erudition and ingenuity.

This thesis was however so eccentric in its point of view that Graves played

down its claims to historical truth by subtitling it 'a historical grammar of poetic myth'. And privately he wrote that "*The White Goddess* is about how poets think: it's not a scientific book . . . Some day scholars will sort out the White Goddess grain from the chaff. It's a crazy book and I didn't mean to write it." Nevertheless

A passion for words
Surrounded by books and paper, Graves works in his study. He was a learned and scholarly man, although unconventional in his views.

Douglas Glass © J. C. Glass

The Writer at Work

Inspirational island

For most of his life Graves made his home on the Mediterranean island of Mallorca. The village of Deyá, where he lived, was described as long ago as 1898 as being notable for 'its collection of strange and eccentric foreigners', but it remained unspoilt by the tourism that blotted other parts of the island. Graves referred to his home as 'Paradise'. Here he felt close not only to nature, but also to myths and to Mallorca's ancient history. It was an environment highly congenial to his particular gifts and interests.

Douglas Glass © J. C. C. Glass

BBC Hulton Picture Library

Tireless craftsman

(left) Few authors have revised their writings as painstakingly as Graves. Successive editions of his Collected Poems show how even after his works were published he continued to think about them and to modify them.

spoken honesty about life in the trenches has assured its enduring popularity.

Fortunately for his readers, Graves' complicated private life meant that he was always in need of money and worked immensely hard at prose as well as verse, though he tended to dismiss the former as a 'sideline'. He was involved in a number of collaborations, most successfully with Alan Hodge. As well as the entertaining social history *The Long Weekend*, they published together *The Reader over Your Shoulder* (1943), advocating a plain, sane prose style and mischievously presenting an anthology of bad writing and sloppy thinking by teachers, clergymen and well-known contemporary writers.

HISTORICAL NOVELS

By the 1930s Robert Graves had become best known as a novelist – ironically so, since he claimed to be lacking in the true novelist's imagination. According to Graves, the majority of his short stories – even the most improbable – were simply accounts of things that had actually hap-

pened. "Pure fiction is beyond my imaginative range; I fetched back the main elements of *The Shout* from a cricket-match at Littlemore Asylum, Oxford."

And, in fact, Graves published only one full-length piece of 'pure' fiction, "my light and eccentric novel *Antigua, Penny, Puce*." All the others were historical novels, for which a factual framework already existed. These range impressively over time – from ancient Greece (*The Golden Fleece*, 1944), through Rome (the Claudius books), Byzantium (*Count Belisarius*, 1938) and 17th-century England (*Wife to Mr Milton*, 1943), to the stories of a British soldier during and after the American War of Independence (*Sergeant Lamb of the Ninth*, 1940; *Proceed, Sergeant Lamb*, 1941) and of 'Palmer the poisoner', whom Graves finds not guilty (*They Hanged My Saintly Billy*, 1957).

Graves' assessment of his creative contribution was singularly humble, however. "My motive or excuse is usually to clear up some historical problem which has puzzled me", was his over-modest way of describing his historical novels, and the Herculean task of reconstructive and detective work involved in them. *I, Claudius* and Graves' other novels are not history, which needs to be regularly rewritten, but works of art that create their own imaginative historical world.

As a teenager Robert Graves devoted himself to poetry, vowing never to compromise his artistic integrity for the sake of commercial or literary fashion. He developed a distinctive style in *The Pier-Glass* (1921), and continued in his own way in the face of an increasingly dominant modernist movement. Meanwhile, he earned his living as a prose-writer.

After the success of his candid autobiography, *Goodbye to All That* (1929), he emerged as an outstanding historical novelist with *I, Claudius* (1934). He continued to vary his output, publishing *Antigua, Penny, Puce* (1936), a wild comedy, and *The Long Week-End* (1940, with Alan Hodge), a social

history of the inter-war years. *King Jesus* (1946) stirred controversy; and the combination of anthropology, guesswork and poetic insight in *The White Goddess* (1948) dazzled some but infuriated others. Over 40 years, Graves published occasional short stories, issued as a collection in 1965, although it is his poetry which is at last seen as central to his life's work.

THE PIER-GLASS
◆ 1921 ◆

Graves' sense of guilt and the difficulty in readjusting after a harrowing World War (below) are reflected in this early collection of poems, notably in *Dawn* and *Reproach*. The title poem is narrated by a woman trapped in a dream and doomed to haunt a 'lost manor'. Her steps always lead her to a bedroom with an old, cracked, 'sullen pier-glass'. Once a servant in the house, she was wronged by her master, and killed him, rather than forgive. Graves identifies strongly with her.

   This collection, Graves' sixth, was the first in which he found his own distinctive voice, encouraged by his friend T. E. Lawrence, to whom the book is dedicated. Graves asked Lawrence's opinion and while Lawrence did not claim to understand the poetry, he nevertheless recognized its merit: 'A good deal of it is rather odd, but I think there can be no two opinions about the excellence of the writing, and much of it is sheer beauty.'

CLAUDIUS THE GOD
◆ 1934 ◆

Claudius' life has been transformed by his marriage to Messalina (right) and his unwilling promotion to Emperor by the Palace Guard. Now he continues his 'autobiography' in this sequel to *I, Claudius*. As Emperor, he is an effective, if unconventional reformer. He initiates the conquest of remote, barbaric Britain. Then he makes a shattering discovery – that his beloved Messalina has been betraying him for years and now plans to overthrow him. Thanks to the faithful Narcissus, Messalina is dealt with; but the effect on Claudius is drastic. He becomes convinced that Rome is so far gone in corruption that only when the city has drowned itself in evil will there be any change for the better. He therefore takes steps to see that Rome degenerates towards ruin. His ultimate positive effort – to save his son Britannicus from the coming disaster – is thwarted, and the pen falls from his hand. But one final posthumous irony completes the Emperor's history.

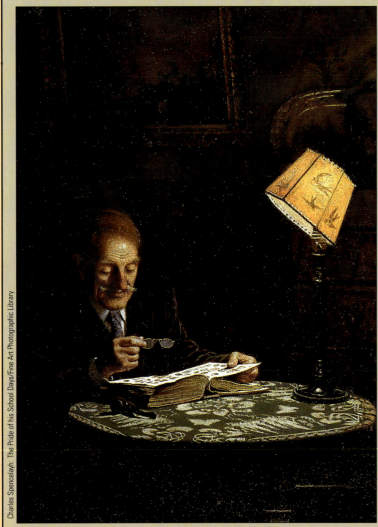

Charles Spencelayh: The Pride of his School Days/Fine Art Photographic Library

ANTIGUA, PENNY, PUCE
◆ 1936 ◆

A valuable Antiguan stamp and the strange obsession of the collector (left) are central to this, Graves' only 'modern' novel. Oliver and Jane Price are brother and sister – and lifelong rivals. Their antagonism comes to rest on the issue of who owns this stamp in their shared childhood collection. Jane is a born 'winner', but initially Oliver gets possession. When he attempts to sell the stamp at auction, Jane interrupts the proceedings with an injunction, and the subsequent court case becomes a *cause célèbre*? Is the stamp Oliver's or Jane's? Or does it belong to Oliver's fiancée Edith, who as a child stole it from her father's safe? And what of the man to whom the stamped letter was addressed? New evidence provides a judgement; but the feud is not over.

THE LONG WEEK-END
◆ 1940 ◆

Graves wrote this 'Social History of Great Britain 1918-1939' in collaboration with his friend Alan Hodge. Hugely ambitious and wide-ranging, the work tackles the events, politics, philosophy, pastimes, literature and art (below) of the between-wars era. It compiles a wealth of entertaining anecdotes, but is genuinely informative in its analysis of the social revolution which threatened – but failed – to materialize after the First World War, during the General Strike and from the Depression. Excavation of Tutankhamen's tomb, the advent of the BBC, the Loch Ness Monster, the Abdication crisis, mah-jong, talking pictures, pacifism, nudism and hiking are all seen as somehow symptomatic of the period.

W. Gale: The Entry Into Jerusalem/Fine Art Photographic Library

Stanley Spencer: The Resurrection, Cookham. Tate Gallery, London

THE WHITE GODDESS
◆ 1948 ◆

The Moon Goddess (right) was held by Graves to be the true muse of poets, and he devoted this work of extraordinary scholarship and speculation to her. Drawing on various cultures centring on the sacrificial, annual killing of kings, Graves theorizes about an Old Stone Age society ruled by female representatives of the Moon Goddess. Sadly, this three-in-one figure of mother, lover and crone was eventually supplanted by Greek and Hebrew father-gods . . .

Edwin Long. Ancient Cyprus/Fine Art Photographic Library

KING JESUS
◆ 1946 ◆

This controversial account of Jesus' life (above) casts him as the son of a temple virgin secretly married to Herod Antipater, whose royal blood he inherits. To break the hold of the pagan 'Mother Goddess', Jesus preaches celibacy but when this fails to win people's minds, he plans to fulfil prophecy by dying at the hand of one of his disciples.

Mary Evans Picture Library

COLLECTED SHORT STORIES
◆ 1965 ◆

Graves made Ancient Rome (left) *his own particular territory*, and several of these stories, written between 1924 and 1962, return there. In *The Myconian*, a naive Greek philosopher is shown such Roman delights as fights at the Colosseum and chariot racing. Similarly, Graves made Mallorca his own literary preserve, and some stories – notably *A Toast to Ava Gardner* – have the island for their setting.

ROMAN GODS AND HEROES

The ancient tales of the gods and goddesses of Olympus have haunted the imagination for centuries, inspiring some of Europe's finest art and literature.

When Robert Graves went to Oxford University, he took up the study of English Literature. After 'fourteen years . . . principally at Latin and Greek' he was, he claimed, 'fed up with the Classics'. The Classics had, however, found their way into his blood and throughout his life Graves continued to respond to the imaginative beauties of the ancient world – beauties that are enshrined particularly in the great body of myth and legend that is one of the ancient world's most profound and enduring legacies to Western civilization. Since the Renaissance it has inspired much of Europe's greatest literature and art, just as it coloured much of Graves' own writing.

SUPERHUMAN BEINGS

Ancient myths are varied in origin. There are stories that have some basis in fact (those about the siege of Troy, for example), embroidered through the ages by imperfect recollection and poetic fancy, and others that might be classified as folklore or popular fiction. The type with which we are most familiar, however, are imaginative stories about gods or superhuman beings, often explaining how some custom or natural phenomenon came into being; the Roman god Neptune,

Love on Olympus
Vulcan, the lame god of fire and a great blacksmith (he sits beside his anvil), wooed and married Venus, the goddess of beauty. But later she cuckolded him with Mars, the god of war.

Ruler of the waves
(below) Neptune, the god who ruled the sea and its inhabitants, is drawn through the waves by white seahorses. He was invoked by sailors to give them a safe voyage, but he could also stir up the sea with his trident and cause storms and shipwrecks when he was angry.

E. K. Brice: Neptune and his Horses/Fine Art Photographic Library

for example (Poseidon is his Greek counterpart), was lord of the sea and was believed to be the cause of shipwrecks, floods and earthquakes.

The religions of the Greeks and Romans were many-layered and differed fundamentally from the chief faiths of the modern world – in fact neither Greek nor Latin has a word that corresponds exactly with the English 'religion' or 'religious'. There was no priestly caste or official creed, no book like the Bible or the Koran to which one can turn for an established body of belief. The Romans in particular borrowed elements freely from the religions of the foreign peoples who formed part of their vast Empire, and there were secret sects and many purely local cults in addition to the 'Establishment' deities. It is not surprising, therefore, that myths often exist in different versions, and that there is much that is confusing or contradictory in classical mythology.

JUPITER'S AMOROUS ADVENTURES

In spite of the varied nature of Roman religion, the major gods and goddesses of the Romans and many of the most famous legends about them were derived directly from the Greeks. It was, however, the Roman poet Ovid (mentioned in *I, Claudius* as going into voluntary exile in Augustus' reign) who was the single most important source for transmitting classical mythology to later ages. His masterpiece, *The Metamorphoses*, is a series of verse tales about mythological characters, linked by the fact that they all deal with the theme of changing shape. The star performer at this trick was undoubtedly Jupiter (Zeus in his Greek form), the king of gods, and his reason for changing shape was usually to escape the jealous attentions of his wife Juno (in Greek Hera) while going about his favourite pursuit of seducing beautiful mortals. In this way he turned himself into a bull to seduce Europa, a swan for Leda, a satyr for Antiope, a shower of gold for Danae and a cloud for Io. Jupiter sometimes took a fancy to boys as well as girls, and he turned himself into an eagle to abduct the beautiful shepherd Ganymede.

Juno did her best to thwart Jupiter's amorous

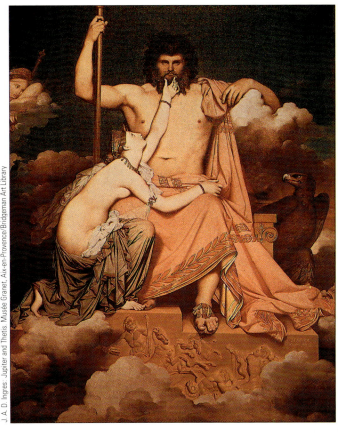

King of the gods
The majestic Jupiter is seen in all his remote Olympian splendour, as the nymph Thetis, the mother of the Greek warrior Achilles, seeks favour for her son.

adventures, and their schemes and counterschemes are best illustrated in the story of Io, the daughter of a king of Argos. Jupiter changed himself into a cloud to hide his infidelity, but Juno was not deceived. Changing tack slightly, Jupiter then turned Io into a white heifer, but Juno saw through this ruse, demanded the animal as a present, and set the hundred-eyed giant Argus to guard it. To recover the unfortunate Io/heifer, Jupiter employed his messenger Mercury (Hermes),

Animal wet nurse
The twins Romulus and Remus, the legendary founders of Rome, were suckled by a wolf and had food brought to them by a woodpecker. Such tales abound in mythology: Jupiter himself was suckled by a goat.

who charmed Argus to sleep with his beautiful playing on the lyre and then cut off his head. Juno took Argus' eyes to decorate the tail of her peacock (a marvellous explanation of how the bird came to have such spectacularly beautifully patterned tail feathers), and in revenge sent a gadfly to torment the hapless Io.

The wranglings of Jupiter and Juno are fairly typical of the escapades of the gods, for although they are represented in Greek, Roman and later art as noble and majestic figures, much of their existence was taken up with lust, jealousy and intrigue in a kind of celestial soap opera. (There was incest, too, for Juno was Jupiter's sister as well as his wife.)

VULCAN'S REVENGE

The most entertaining of the many stories of the tangled love life on Mount Olympus (the home of the gods) concerns Venus (Aphrodite), the goddess of beauty and love, and Mars (Ares), the god of war and son of Jupiter and Juno. Venus was married to Vulcan (Hephaestus), the lame god of fire, but she had an affair with Mars, a brutal character who was otherwise disliked by virtually everyone, including his parents. The sun god Sol (Helios) reported the infidelity to Vulcan, who

Wisdom and war
Minerva (above, centre) is primarily known as the goddess of wisdom and as the patroness of the arts and learning. She was also, however, associated with war – hence the helmet that she habitually wears. Here she is shown surrounded by philosophers and soldiers – two greatly contrasting professions who came under her protection.

Seduced by a swan
Leda, the wife of King Tyndareus of Sparta, was one of Jupiter's many illicit human lovers. He changed himself into a swan to make love to her, in the hope of avoiding the jealous attentions of his wife Juno.

used his marvellous skills as a blacksmith to take his revenge. He made a net that was so fine it was invisible but so strong it was unbreakable, and secretly fixed it to the adulterers' bed, so next time they made love they were trapped in it. The other gods were called on to witness their shame, although Mercury rather tactlessly remarked that he would not mind being in the same position as Mars.

When, in the narrative of Graves' novel, Claudius is asked to act as a bouncer at a royal brothel, he carries out his duties with such panache that Caligula dubs him Vulcan. Like the god, he has a clumsy, unexpected cunning, and Claudius is not at all displeased by the comparison.

'TO THE FAIREST'

The theme of the revenge of a thwarted deity had more dire consequences in the story of the Judgement of Paris. Paris was a shepherd who married the daughter of the river god Oeneus. Discordia (Eris), the goddess of strife, was the only one of the gods not invited to the wedding, so to stir up trouble she threw a golden apple inscribed 'To the fairest' among the guests. Juno, Venus and Minerva (Athena), the goddess of wisdom, each claimed the apple, and Jupiter ordered Paris to make the choice. Paris was subjected to outrageous bribery from the three contestants in this celestial beauty competition, and he succumbed to Venus' offer to reward him with the love of any woman in the world. The woman he chose was Helen, the wife of Menelaus, king of Sparta, whose beauty Venus described in the most rapturous terms.

Paris abducted Helen and carried her off to Troy – he had been born the son of Priam, king of Troy, but left to die as a child because his mother had dreamed he would cause the destruction of the city. The dream came true, for the abduction of Helen started the Trojan War, which resulted, after a siege of ten years, in the city being sacked. Two great poems of the ancient world – Homer's *Iliad* and Virgil's *Aeneid* – tell the story of the Trojan War and how the gods took the sides of various warriors and controlled their destinies. Aeneas, a Trojan prince, was under the special protection of Jupiter, and after the destruction of the city he

escaped and eventually founded the colony from which Rome grew. The distinction of founding the city itself is accorded to his descendants Romulus and Remus, twins who were reared by a wolf after they had survived an attempt to drown them at birth. Their mother was a Vestal Virgin who had been ravished by Mars and thrown into prison for being 'unchaste'.

Another famous pair of twins – Castor and Pollux – show that the dividing line between gods and mortals was sometimes a very fine one. According to the best-known account, they were the sons of Leda, a queen of Sparta, and Jupiter, who made

Beauty and the beast
(right) Artists often depict Venus and Mars in various scenes from their extra-marital affair. But here the god and goddess are used rather as timeless symbols expressing the power of beauty and love (Venus) to conquer strife (the brutal Mars).

S. H. Meteyard: Venus and Mars/Fine Art Photographic Library

love to her in the form of a swan – appropriately they were hatched from an egg. They became famous for their athletic prowess and were among the Argonauts who accompanied Jason on his epic voyage to find the Golden Fleece. After one of the brothers' most celebrated exploits – carrying off the daughters of their uncle Leucippus, who were betrothed to another set of twins – Castor, who was mortal, was killed. Pollux begged Jupiter to allow him and his brother to alternate life and death, one living for a day in the heavens and the other in the underworld, and then exchanging roles the next day. Jupiter agreed and later transformed them into the constellation Gemini (the twins), one of the signs of the Zodiac.

HELPERS OF MANKIND

Castor and Pollux were worshipped as helpers of mankind, and in particular were said to protect sailors in peril at sea. They were also appealed to by soldiers going into battle, and a cult developed for them in Rome, with a large temple dedicated to their worship in the Forum (the great public square) in the 5th century BC.

The attitude of mortals towards the gods was, however, not always one of reverence. In *I, Claudius*, the raving Caligula challenges Neptune to combat, shouting, "you treacherously

Labour pains
In one of the fits of madness sent by Juno, Hercules – the product of her husband's extra-marital amours – killed his own children. In penance he had to serve King Eurystheus of Tiryns for twelve years, undertaking any task asked of him. Hercules successfully accomplished the twelve great Labours appointed to him, including slaying the Hydra, a multi-headed monster (left). The vengeful Juno sent a crab to hinder Hercules by biting his foot.

Mary Evans Picture Library

Sources and Inspiration

wrecked my father's fleet". He orders his soldiers to attack the sea with their weapons (rock-hurling catapults as well as arrows and swords). "Neptune made no attempt to defend himself or reply", Graves explains playfully, "except that one man was nipped by a lobster and another stung by a jelly-fish."

In spite of such un-Olympian behaviour, by the time of Claudius the Romans had begun to accord the status of gods to their Emperors, although some people frowned on the practice. In *I, Claudius*, when the deification of the recently deceased Emperor Augustus is being considered, Gallus says, "It was all very well to decree new gods to ignorant Asiatic provincials, but the honourable House [the Senate] ought to pause before ordering educated citizens to worship one of their own number."

GREATEST OF HEROES

The cause of Augustus' deification is supported by Atticus, a senior magistrate, who "solemnly rose to say that when Augustus' corpse had been burned on Mars Field he had seen a cloud descending from heaven and the dead man's spirit then ascending on it, precisely in the way in which tradition relates that the spirits of Romulus and Hercules ascended. He would swear by all the Gods that he was testifying the truth."

The appeal to the example of Hercules (Herakles) was an important one, for he was the most popular of ancient heroes and the only mortal who had been raised after his death to the same status as the supreme Olympian gods. He started life with a great advantage for a hero, for although his mother Alcema was a mortal, his father was Jupiter. It was clear he was cut out for great things

On cloud nine
Jupiter was highly inventive in disguising himself to hide his infidelities with mortals from his wife Juno. Here, changed into a cloud, he is rapturously embraced by Io, but Juno later made her pay for her pleasure.

Apple of discord
This divine beauty contest, known as The Judgement of Paris, is one of the most popular mythological subjects in art, not least because it gave painters such a wonderful opportunity of displaying their skill in depicting beautiful female nudes. Paris, the handsomest of mortals, presents the prize of a golden apple to Venus, whom he has declared more beautiful than Juno (left) or Minerva. Venus had bribed him with the offer of the love of Helen of Troy, who Paris later abducted, thus starting the Trojan War.

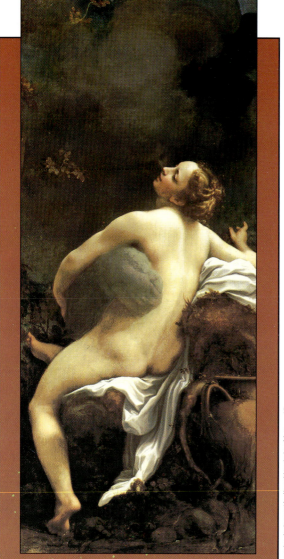

when – still a baby in his cradle – he strangled the pair of poisonous snakes that the ever-jealous Juno had sent to kill him.

The rest of Hercules' earthly life was taken up with similar prodigious feats of strength and heroism, triumphing over evil against heavy odds, although he also found time to indulge a sexual appetite that proved him a true son of Jupiter's. He was renowned for his generous, open nature, but he was also subject to fits of madness, when his rage was murderous. At his death (which was brought about by trickery), Jupiter hurled a thunderbolt to consume his funeral pyre and he was carried to Olympus in a chariot by Minerva.

IMMORTALS OF OLYMPUS

The legends of Hercules are so vivid and so memorable that he has inspired a host of writers and artists, and as he is only one of the immortals of Olympus it is not surprising that classical mythology has continued to haunt the European imagination. To the modern reader, these marvellous stories are often approached through Robert Graves' book *The Greek Myths* (1955), which opens the door to a timeless world of adventure, wonder and enchantment.

H. E. BATES

✦ 1905-1974 ✦

One of the great English storytellers, H. E. Bates wove his art
from the tiniest and most unlikely shreds of inspiration. He was
discovered at the age of 20 and steered towards professionalism
by the finest of mentors. His talent withstood ill health and
changing fashions, and enabled him to make the leap into the
modern world of film and radio. But he remained a
countryman first and foremost, immortalizing the particular
English landscape he knew so well with his sensuous prose.

A RURAL SPIRIT

**Shaped and succoured by the everyday life of a rural community,
H. E. Bates found his world abruptly expanded by fame, war
and travel. But he always remained true to his English roots.**

Bates fondly described his family as 'simple country folk', yet despite his later literary success, he made no serious attempt to leap from their world to a more dazzling one filled with celebrities and literati. Bates' first loves, the countryside and ordinary people, remained the core ingredients of both his life and his fiction.

BOOT BOYS

Herbert Ernest Bates was born on 16 May 1905, at Rushden, in the Nene Valley, Northamptonshire. His formative years were most significantly shaped by his grandfather and father. The latter endowed him with a love for literature and music, the former with a profound feeling for Nature. Both men worked in a local shoe factory, as did Bates' mother, Lucy, who taught him self-reliance and discipline. The family were ardent Methodists and might attend church five times on a Sunday – one consequence of which was that the young Bates grew up with a strong animosity towards organized religion.

In compensation, Rushden had the advantage of beautiful country walks, and Bates also had the chance to join in farm work at harvest time. Such was the pull of the outdoor world that Bates was intensely bored by school, although he was no intellectual slouch. As the brightest in the class, he was given a separate desk and a specially tailored curriculum and, in his own words, he 'soared away' to academic excellence.

In those days, his sights were set on becoming an artist and he took sixpenny lessons from a lady art teacher. His other spare time was filled with football, cricket and reading. Bates' father owned an enormous stock of novels, including those by Sir Arthur Conan Doyle, Rudyard Kipling and J. M. Barrie. And a couple of years before leaving school at 16½, he discovered his true vocation. Asked to write an essay on Shakespeare by an enterprising new teacher, he 'suddenly knew, incontestably that [he] was or was going to be a writer'. From now on he devoured even more books, extending his reading to Milton's prose and the Authorized Version of the Bible.

When he left school, he was 'naïve, extremely gauche and extremely sensitive'. He obtained work as a junior reporter on a local paper, but the daily diet of weddings and rural trivia bored him. Clearly not a budding journalist, Bates resigned and was faced with a bleak future. His next job, unpromising as it seemed, was to prove very useful, for it provided invaluable time.

Now aged 17, Bates began work as a clerk in a leather factory. But there was so little work to do, once the day's orders had been sorted out, that he was free to write. He later described his first effort at a novel as a 'shapeless, amateurish, useless

'Oh! how we walked. Winter and summer we tramped . . . the footpaths, the blackberry hedges, the river towpaths, the woodland ridings . . . my father striding out athletically.' Thus Bates grew to love the countryside (above).

Rushden, Northants 'A palpably dreadful mess of that mixture of blue slate, factory, chapel and that harsh Midland red brick which equally oppresses the heart, soul, eye and senses.' Bates' description of his home town (left) shows less affection than he felt for the 'dry, droll, unshaven independence' of its inhabitants. Most worked at the town's many shoe factories: 'I became very proud of my shoemakers', recalled Bates, who styled his fictional Evensford on Rushden.

Courtesy of Mrs H. E. Bates

monster'. But with his next, *The Two Sisters,* again written in the warehouse, he struck gold.

A year passed before the third and final draft was ready, in 1925, to send off to London publishers. But before their response, he was fired from the warehouse and, at a time of appalling joblessness, collected unemployment benefit. He put his enforced idleness to good use, however, reading short-story writers such as Chekhov, Maupassant, Gorki and Flaubert.

Meanwhile, at a party, Bates met an attractive, quick-witted 17-year-old, Marjorie ('Madge') Cox. Years before, his grandfather had actually saved Madge's life, dashing into her family's cottage one night to save the child when the nearby shoe factory had burst into flames. Bates' joy at meeting her was increased by a generous reply from the publishers Jonathan Cape: they were offering to publish his novel for the then-excellent sum of £25. To his amusement, they assumed the

Summer delights
Young H. E., his mother and baby sister are pictured above at the annual town picnic on Rushden's 'Wesleyan Tea Field'. Harvest found him in the fields (below). (Bates is the child at the foot of the ladder.)

Courtesy of Mrs H. E. Bates

Threshing - Small Holdings, Higham

Key Dates
1905 born Rushden, Northamptonshire
1925 first novel, *The Two Sisters*
1931 marries Madge Cox; moves to Kent
1941 joins RAF and writes under the name Flying Officer X
1944 *Fair Stood the Wind for France*
1945 posted to India
1952 *Love for Lydia*
1969-72 three-volume autobiography
1973 awarded CBE
1974 dies at Canterbury

author was a woman, and had addressed the letter to 'Miss Bates'.

The London meeting with Cape's directors and reader was momentous. Not only did it launch Bates' literary career, but it also introduced him to his future advisor and friend Edward Garnett. Garnett gave Bates the tough, incisive criticism that this raw, largely self-taught young man so badly needed, and turned him from a sporadically talented writer into a consistently good one. Garnett also helped Bates through many financial crises, and found ready markets for his short stories among his various literary contacts.

This and subsequent visits to London were the first taste Bates had really had of life beyond the Nene Valley. He was initially delighted by it. By contrast, the world back home suddenly seemed like a 'totally negative wasteland'. But there was worse disillusionment to come: Madge rejected his proposal of marriage.

Bates moved south to London to work in a

A trip to London
At the tender age of 20 (right), Bates was invited up to London (centre) to meet Jonathan Cape, the publisher who had accepted his first novel. At a sophisticated, literary lunch in Soho, Bates felt out of his depth. But his "innocent struggle with the parmesan" paled into insignificance against his next encounter – when his hero, Cape's reader, Edward Garnett entered the restaurant he was overwhelmed.

Fact or Fiction

RUSHDEN HALL

As he wrote *Love for Lydia*, Bates drew on the memory of a visit to Rushden Hall some 30 years before as a reporter. He had 'the strangest feeling that the shaping Divinity had actually sent me there for a purpose'. At about the same time, Bates glimpsed a beautiful girl in a pony-trap. Time fused these events: the girl became Lydia, the Hall the home of the Aspens.

David Hall

---

bookshop, heartened afresh by the encouraging reviews of *The Two Sisters* and a new friendship – with the pianist Harriet Cohen. The two almost immediately formed a close bond. Harriet was eager to flirt, but not to take the relationship any further. She filled the void left by Madge and introduced him to the leading artists of the day. But a London lifestyle was not for Bates, and he soon returned to Rushden – to dancing, cricket and football, and to tackling a more ambitious, longer novel: *The Voyagers*. It was a bad point in his life which he later dismissed as a 'literary penal servitude'. He had little money and was terrified that his new novel was not going to shape up.

SHAKEN AWAKE
When Bates finished *The Voyagers,* he was so 'utterly exhausted' that he went to Germany for his first trip abroad. But he did not complete his itinerary because an affectionate letter from Madge sent him hurrying back to England. More than just Madge was waiting for him.

Edward Garnett had read *The Voyagers* and was not pleased. He rejected it as 'an utter absolute disaster'. Bates later recalled how 'that morning [Edward] hit me with everything he'd got'. Though dismayed, Bates knew Garnett was right and was quickly aware that the criticism was aimed at freeing the real artist in him. As Bates wrote in his autobiography, Garnett's attack 'in the finest sense . . . woke me'.

The best of Bates' social life centred on The Cearne, Edward Garnett's stone cottage on the North Downs of Sussex. A typical weekend included a visit from T. E. Lawrence (of Arabia) who biked up from Dorset for tea. Such company was stimulating and, meanwhile, there were trips to London for the theatre and concerts.

Now, in his mid-twenties, Bates married Madge. Once, as a child, glimpsing Kent through a train window, he had been struck by the 'strong impression that somehow this was my second home'. And true to his premonition, Bates now moved to Kent where he and Madge bought a

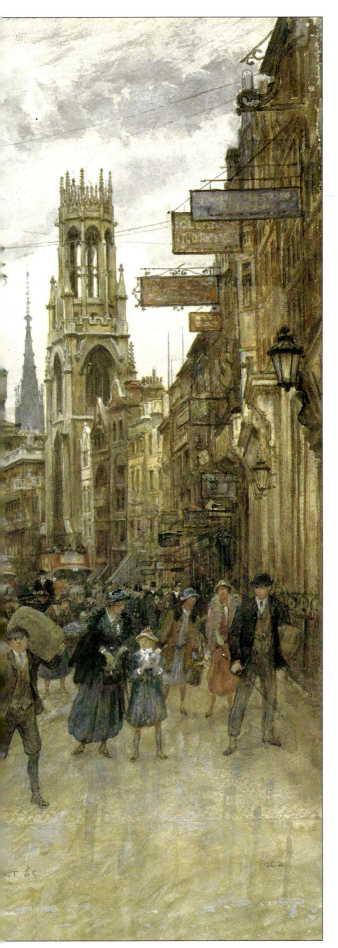

Popperfoto

Man of cultivation
*Bates was never so happy
as when he was in his
garden (above). He wrote
several gardening books.*

Joining the few
*A year after witnessing
the Battle of Britain
(below), Bates became
the official 'voice' of the
RAF pilot, writing stories
based on the men's tough,
courageous lives.*

derelict granary. Here, 'while Madge attacked the
house and its domestic affairs', Bates began hew-
ing a garden from the wildly overgrown farm-
yard. It was to be his constant joy and solace, as
he created and worked at his vision over the next
40 years.

Meanwhile the Bates lived on £2 a week, and
soon they were expecting a first child. Where a
lack of money had previously been a problem, it
now became a nightmare. Bates worked 'like hell',
writing short stories in the morning, articles in the
afternoon and reviews in the evening. His
remorseless schedule resulted in one alarming
blackout when, wandering the streets of London

Paul Nash: Battle of Britain/Imperial War Museum

for an hour or so, he did not know who or where he was.

However, Bates' relentless work did pay off with two successful pieces, *The Mill* and *The Fallow Land*. Throughout the rest of his twenties he struggled to get by financially, and became increasingly prone to severe attacks of abdominal pain and 'always . . . the fear of drying up, of greater debts, of failures and rejections'.

Edward Garnett's death in 1937 devastated Bates, but by now he knew that he had acquired the instincts of a novelist. He was proved right when *Spella Ho,* his next work, was reprinted three times in a year. The money from this work and from the American publishers (who asked him to the United States to serialize it) made him financially secure for the first time in his life. But private success was suddenly countered by public terror. Bates returned to an England on the brink of World War II.

FLYING OFFICER X

Bates and Madge determined to take a last look at Europe before the conflagration: they visited Yugoslavia and Italy, and returned invigorated. Meanwhile, Garnett's son David had taken over as Cape's reader and was waiting to lacerate Bates for spawning a second 'monster' (a novel of 'almost unrelieved melancholy' about a war widow). Fortunately, David also knew how to tinge criticism with encouragement, so that Bates was soon hard at work again, writing more short stories and a survey of the genre.

With a growing family to support, Bates accepted the post of literary editor of the *Spectator* magazine. But he was unsuited to the job and was eventually fired. In 1941 he was given a commission in the RAF's 'Public Relations Department' as a short-story writer. Given the nominal rank of squadron-leader, he was allowed a degree of freedom to observe most aspects of a pilot's life, but was not allowed to risk his own, which meant flying missions were ruled out. Nonetheless, he found no shortage of material. His first piece con-

Family man
Bates' family is pictured above watching him play cricket: Madge right, his parents and his four children. He revelled in the Kent countryside (above) and its rural pursuits.

Screen success
Film adaptations of such books as The Purple Plain *(below) brought financial comfort to an author already rich in reputation.*

cerned an officer's awful duty of informing a pilot's relatives that he has been killed in action. Bates' superiors were so impressed with his work that he was given the grand pseudonym of Flying Officer X and, using the name, he now tackled *Fair Stood the Wind for France.*

Bates' spell in the RAF was hallmarked by bouts of stomach pain, and the psychological anguish of watching German doodle bugs (pilotless planes packed with explosives) scream across the Kent skyline towards London. Later he was given the opportunity of travelling to France to inspect the launch sites. He also went further afield – to Malta, Italy, Cairo, Calcutta and Burma. All the while he was storing up incidents and characters for his future fictions.

Bates returned home in 1945 but was at once paralyzed with fear that he could not write. The

GREGORY PECK
The Purple Plain
MAURICE DENHAM · LYNDON BROOK · BRENDA DE BANZIE
WIN MIN THAN
COLOUR BY TECHNICOLOR

Mike Busselle/Photographers Library

EDWARD GARNETT

Edward Garnett wrote volumes of fiction and non-fiction, but his great contribution to literature lay elsewhere. As reader to the leading publishing house, Jonathan Cape, he discovered and encouraged some of Britain's greatest writers. Bates thought his first meeting with Garnett, in 1925, was a crucial day in his life. The two became close friends, Garnett giving Bates time, constructive (but often savage) criticism, and encouragement. He, his wife, and the son who later took over his post at Cape, lived in spartan rigour at a stone cottage called The Cearne. Here eminent authors often met and talked.

It is impossible to overstate Garnett's importance as a friend and mentor. Bates wrote, 'I have got a monument up to you inside me.' Three years after Garnett's death in 1947, Bates produced a biography of this most distinguished literary figure.

East had a crippling effect, a 'catastrophic impact . . . on his sensitivity' prompted by the 'callous contempt for life' he witnessed there. The only way out was to exorcise everything he had heard and seen by writing about it. The results were two highly successful books: *The Purple Plain* and *The Jacaranda Tree.*

GOING INTO PICTURES

In 1947 Bates' abdominal pains had reached such intensity that his doctors decided he had suffered an internal haemorrhage and operated at last. They had to remove most of his stomach, but he was free of agony for the first time in years.

Three years later came his fine semi-autobiographical novel *Love for Lydia* and a batch of radio plays. Still acutely sensitive to criticism, his writing nearly came to an end after the scathing remarks of a friend on his work, *The Sleepless Moon.* But he was quickly rescued by his love for the short-story form and by the intervention of the film world. Fellow writer A. E. Coppard encouraged him to use 'cinematic' techniques in his writing – fade-outs, cuts and close-ups. The American director Leslie Fenton was so excited by the Flying Officer X stories that he asked Bates to turn them into filmscripts, which he agreed to do, questioning his success in retrospect.

Another great fan of Bates was the director/producer Alexander Korda, who gave him a lavish salary and introduced him to the film director David Lean. Soon afterwards, Lean bought the rights to *Fair Stood the Wind for France* and *The Purple Plain,* giving Gregory Peck the lead role in the latter. He also sent Bates and Madge to Fiji, Samoa and Tahiti in search of inspiration.

When Bates returned to England, however, he launched into a thoroughly British venture, intro-

Ripe old age
In contrast to many great writers, Bates knew more joy in his old age than his youth. His health was better, and his achievements were crowned by the award of a CBE (Commander of the British Empire) in 1973. His children and grandchildren he called 'a handsome cornucopia'; the countryside still held its mystical spell, and his talents were undimmed.

ducing readers to his most memorable creations, the Larkin family, inhabitants of a 'perfick' world. The Larkins achieved best-seller popularity in *The Darling Buds of May* and *A Breath of Fresh Air.* All the while, Bates' imagination was toying with people and incidents and stories from long ago. *The Triple Echo* sprang from an idea he had been nursing for nearly 25 years. Again, Bates' highly cinematic style (perhaps a result of his early love for painting) paid off. The story, published in 1978, was turned into a highly acclaimed film.

In Bates' final years, he turned his mind to an autobiography, issued in three volumes: *The Vanished World, The Blossoming World* and *The World in Ripeness.* By now, he was such an invaluable part of the English story-telling tradition that in 1973 he was awarded the CBE. He died the following year, aged 68, in Canterbury.

P. Ward/Daily Telegraph Colour Library

LOVE FOR LYDIA

In this poignant tale, Bates captures the ecstasy and acute sadness of first love, charting the bitter-sweet lives of young people linked by both fate and friendship.

*L*ove for Lydia unfolds slowly and painfully to reveal all the intensity and passion of a first love affair. Set in a small town at the end of the 1920s, the feelings aroused by Lydia in all the people she encounters contrast sharply with the stultifying atmosphere of the town. Lydia is charismatic and beautiful, and the devotion she inspires in her admirers is described with a haunting nostalgic quality, making this one of the most moving and memorable of H. E. Bates' novels.

GUIDE TO THE PLOT

Richardson, the 19-year-old narrator of the story, loathes his job as a young newspaper reporter. Sent to the imposing Aspen house for a story, he meets Lydia for the first time. On the death of her father, Lydia's two ageing aunts have brought her to live with them and are anxious that she should have friends and enjoy herself. At their request Richardson takes Lydia skating one Saturday afternoon. She loves it and soon they skate as

often as possible, and at Lydia's insistence, visit every sleazy café and eating house Evensford has to offer.

Lydia rapidly emerges from her shy awkward adolescence, thirsty for new experiences. Her growing sexual curiosity inflames Richardson's passion, and he feels certain, during their mad hot summer together, that he will love her forever. He changes his job, taking an undemanding position as clerk in a small leather firm, from which he escapes each afternoon to meet Lydia clandestinely

> *"She laughed again lying with her mouth across my face, her voice warm with tenderness and rather hoarse, and I felt all summer spin together… into what was really for me a monstrously simple, monstrously complex web of happiness."*

Niels H. Christiansen: Skaters in a frozen winter landscape/Private Collection/Bridgeman Art Library

"A wonderful *time*"

The unfamiliar thrill of company her own age transforms Lydia – almost overnight – into a dazzling coquette.

Guildhall Library, City of London/Bridgeman Art Library

in the summer house on the Aspen estate.

During the winter months he and Lydia go dancing with four other friends. But their regular outings in a chauffeur-driven car gradually turn sour, as Lydia becomes increasingly aware of her sexual power. Alex, one of the four, falls desperately in love with her, and her flirtation with Blackie Johnson, their driver, sends Alex into a jealous frenzy. Drunk and depressed he confides to Richardson, "I keep getting a feeling something bloody awful is going to happen."

Lydia is determined to make sure that her 21st birthday party is an event that Evensford will never forget. In a typically extravagant gesture she invites the whole town, determined that no-one should be left out. Fearing Lydia is growing away from him, Richardson proposes to her at the party. She turns him down, impatiently straining to return to her guests who have begun to sing 'For she's a jolly good fellow . . .' Lydia is at her most powerful; propelled by her desire for danger and excitement, she searches to make further conquests, and inflicts deep suffering on both Alex and Richardson.

On the way home from a Midsummer's Eve party Alex falls from a bridge and drowns. How it all happened and who was to blame is never really clear. Richardson comments:

". . . Alex had been killed not so much by a

fall from a bridge as by an accumulative process of little things, of which some were gay, some stupid, some accidental but all of small importance in themselves. Perhaps he had died on the icy evening when Lydia had first taken notice of Blackie . . ."

Richardson becomes a recluse, unable to bear seeing Lydia or his friends. He meets her again later that summer, and watches painfully as she and Tom (his oldest friend) fall in love. Tragedy strikes again and Richardson flees to London, turning his back on Lydia and Evensford. When he returns two years later every-

Aspen house

(above) The mystique of Evensford's 'big house' acquires an exciting, sensuous glamour for Richardson. It is the setting for his and Lydia's discovery of their own – and each other's – sexuality.

ILN Picture Library

Broadening horizons

(left) Richardson and Lydia are drawn together by her new-found passion for skating, and his growing fascination with her. He neglects his work so that he can meet her every day – "I suddenly did not care about anything but the skating, the frost . . . and the girl in the cloak and the scarlet sweater."

Night owls

(right) Under the fatherly care of their chauffeur, Johnson, Lydia, Richardson and their circle embark on a series of outings – drinking and dancing till the early hours.

ILN Picture Library

thing has changed. With hindsight and a dawning maturity he begins to understand the events of the past and look forward to a new spring and a happier future.

PASTORAL LOVE STORY

Love for Lydia is essentially a brilliantly crafted love story containing many ingredients of a fine mystery, which makes the book a compelling read. Written in the first person, it is fictional autobiography of the best kind. Richardson, the narrator, tells of his love for Lydia as he remembers it, with all the pain and glory he endures over the brief two years of their acquaintance. His story is punctuated with ominous warnings – "I could not tell, then, what was going to happen . . ." – which add a dramatic sense of foreboding to the tale. Even in the most lyrical slow-moving sections of the novel, there is an awareness of tragedy in store – a device guaranteed to maintain suspense.

Love for Lydia is also in a sense a pastoral eulogy. The vivid descriptions of seasonal changes in the landscape surrounding Evensford are bound up with

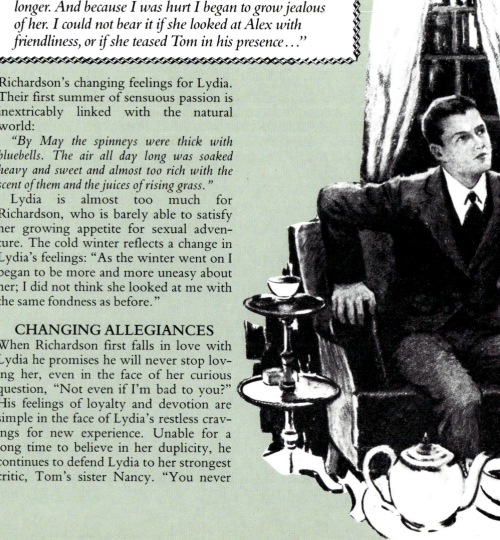

Bernard Fleetwood Walker: Amity/Wolverhampton Art Gallery/Bridgeman Art Library

Old friends
(left) Richardson finds that he is outgrowing the simple, wholesome affection of Nancy, the sister of Tom, his oldest friend. He feels, in knowing Lydia, that he has risen "into a world that I thought was golden and lofty and too complicated for her to understand". But he misjudges Nancy, for she sees some things far more clearly than he does . . .

New passions
(below) As Lydia begins to find other men attractive, Richardson wants her all the more.

In the Background

THE DEPRESSION

The effects of the Wall Street Crash were felt worldwide, reaching Britain within a year. The drop in demand for raw materials forced industry to contract, and by 1932 three million people were unemployed. In *Love for Lydia*, Evensford, which depends on the leather industry, is hit by the slump. Three tanneries close, and four thousand lose their jobs, as if "a million people had suddenly decided to wear shoes no longer."

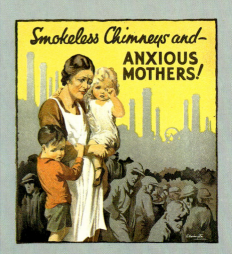

Smokeless Chimneys and ANXIOUS MOTHERS!

"I was hurt because she did not belong to me alone any longer. And because I was hurt I began to grow jealous of her. I could not bear it if she looked at Alex with friendliness, or if she teased Tom in his presence…"

Richardson's changing feelings for Lydia. Their first summer of sensuous passion is inextricably linked with the natural world:
"By May the spinneys were thick with bluebells. The air all day long was soaked heavy and sweet and almost too rich with the scent of them and the juices of rising grass."
Lydia is almost too much for Richardson, who is barely able to satisfy her growing appetite for sexual adventure. The cold winter reflects a change in Lydia's feelings: "As the winter went on I began to be more and more uneasy about her; I did not think she looked at me with the same fondness as before."

CHANGING ALLEGIANCES

When Richardson first falls in love with Lydia he promises he will never stop loving her, even in the face of her curious question, "Not even if I'm bad to you?" His feelings of loyalty and devotion are simple in the face of Lydia's restless cravings for new experience. Unable for a long time to believe in her duplicity, he continues to defend Lydia to her strongest critic, Tom's sister Nancy. "You never even begin to see why women do things do you?" says Nancy scathingly, as Lydia dances outrageously one night in a glamorous scarlet gown.

The centre stage of the novel is Lydia's. Nancy's unrequited love for Richardson, and Pheley the farm girl's attachment to Tom are tragedies in themselves, with their share of misunderstanding, heartache and pain. But every character in the story is in some way subordinate to Lydia, affected by the sheer force of her personality.

Richardson is slow to react to Lydia's faithlessness, preferring instead to cling to the memory of their first months together. He describes his state as "a monstrously simple, monstrously complex web of happiness." Later again, at Lydia's birthday party, he says, "I was caught up . . . tangled and lost, in the most trembling, bemusing web . . ." This aspect of Richardson as a trapped victim of Lydia's devouring nature is hinted at repeatedly throughout the book. Her desire "to be loved – near and far and always and everywhere" is all-consuming, destroying hopes and dreams and ultimately human

Mary Evans Picture Library

lives in its heedless, unrepentant progress.

Inevitably Richardson falls prey to overwhelming feelings of fear and jealousy: "Then I remembered how Alex had kissed her; I remembered the keen stab of jealousy, then sudden slitting through of my puffed vanity; and I was sick because I did not want another person to touch her, and because I did not want to share her with another soul." His behaviour towards her becomes childlike and possessive. His repeated attempts to assert his supremacy in her life irritate Lydia, and she abandons him to his deep sense of pain and loss.

SELF-DISCOVERY

As Lydia changes and develops throughout the story, so too does Richardson. Permeating his version of events is a strong desire not just to record what happened but to understand how and why. During his first encounter with Lydia he felt "poised on the edge of a knife, in a queer excruciating quiver of heat and cold . . ." What makes her exciting is also what makes her dangerous. It takes Richardson a long time to realize Lydia attaches no moral sense to her actions: ". . . she was one of those people who, as they rush into maturity, really think less and less and less. Thought is driven out by a growing automatism of instinct and feeling and blood." She says much later in defence of herself, "People do all sorts of

Changing partners
(above) In the course of one year, Lydia and her friends cross each other's paths in love as well as on the dance floor.

odd things and they never know why."

Richardson believes for a long time that Lydia was deliberately cruel to him. In growing up he finds himself able to forgive her "expressive friendliness with us all", and to admit he had "forgotten how much a prisoner she had been: how exciting and unbalancing and lovely it must have been for that winter to live a life broadening to full freedom with young people like us." Harder to accept is that when Lydia makes her choice of lover she does not choose him.

In his pain and despair at not having Lydia all to himself Richardson chooses solitude for a time, cutting himself off from his friends and family. When he returns to Evensford after two years, he is still restless and unable to settle. It is only after he sees Lydia again and comes to know her in a different way that some meaning reappears in his life – perhaps most significantly in the form of self-knowledge:

"I had so often thought of her growing up from something awkward and lonely that it had not occurred to me that I too had been growing up, just as painfully, in that same way. It had not occurred to me that the pain of love might be part of its flowering."

ILN Picture Library

CHARACTERS IN FOCUS

The characters in *Love for Lydia* are drawn from a wide range of backgrounds. Aristocratic Lydia is fascinated by the brooding physical presence of working-class Blackie. Alex and Richardson share similar intellectual and cultural values, while Tom and Nancy are firmly rooted in a simple farming tradition. Lydia draws all the characters together, but also drives them apart.

WHO'S WHO

Richardson The narrator of the story, sensitive, dreamy and romantic, whose love for Lydia becomes obsessive.

Lydia Aspen A captivating, wealthy young beauty, a "prisoner" of her upbringing who is liberated through her friendship with Richardson.

Alex Sanderson One of Richardson's closest friends – handsome, charming and urbane, even when drunk.

Tom Holland A local farmer's son, Richardson's "oldest friend, as decent and solid and lovable as earth". He is the shyest of Lydia's suitors.

Nancy Holland Tom's devoted sister, "fresh and clean and smooth . . . neither flat nor exciting", she is hopelessly in love with Richardson.

Blackie Johnson The sullen, enigmatic chauffeur who takes Richardson and friends to parties.

The Misses Aspen Lydia's aunts, Miss Bertie and Miss Juliana, who bring her to the Aspen house when her father dies. Kindly and eccentric, they want her to lead a 'normal' life with friends her age.

Captain Rollo Aspen Lydia's sinister uncle, "a thinnish hooked man of six feet with a pronounced weakness of chest and loose in-bred lips".

Mrs Sanderson Alex's mother shows "an almost impulsive refiring of youth that is more beautiful than youthfulness".

Caroline Holmes

A callow youth, Richardson (left) appears the more vulnerable for believing himself to be worldly wise. In his romantic yearning for Lydia, he desires her "as I had always longed . . . in the appalling drabness of an Evensford winter, for the intensified tenderness . . . of a summer day".

Behind an ironical, casually elegant façade, Alex (below) is "inconsistent, excitable, charmingly unreliable, and volatile". A heart-breaker himself, he falls under Lydia's spell, and quite uncharacteristically intends proposing to her. But tragedy intervenes . . .

Arrogant, defensive and inarticulate, the hired chauffeur Blackie (right) a striking contrast to the other young men in Lydia's life. Powerful in appearance and "remarkably dark, . . . with a heavy crop of oiled black hair", he has a magnetic male presence that fascinates Lydia, and infuriates Richardson and Alex. The young men's hostility towards Blackie contributes to one of the decisive tragedies that occurs among their group.

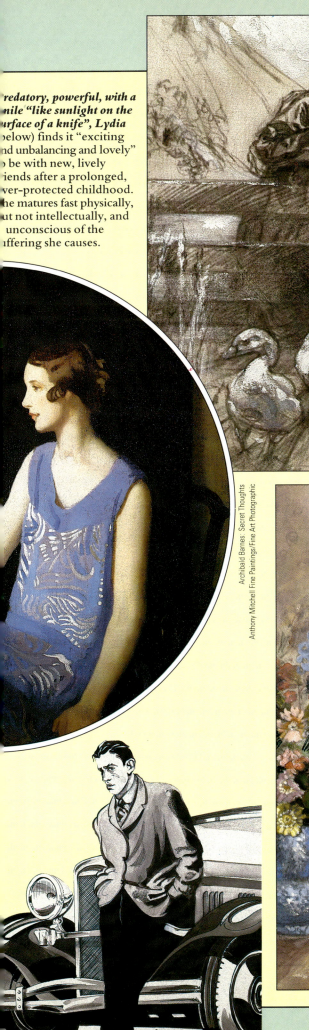

Archibald Barnes: Secret Thoughts
Anthony Mitchell Fine Paintings/Fine Art Photographic

redatory, powerful, with a
nile "like sunlight on the
urface of a knife", Lydia
below) finds it "exciting
nd unbalancing and lovely"
 be with new, lively
iends after a prolonged,
ver-protected childhood.
he matures fast physically,
ut not intellectually, and
 unconscious of the
ffering she causes.

Tom (left) – "big and easy" . . . "a
beautiful swimmer and a good tennis
player, heavy but never rough,
immensely healthy and shy and
warm-hearted " – restores
Richardson's faith in human nature.
Richardson also derives much
comfort from working on the land
with Tom. Then he becomes an
unwilling witness to Tom's growing
feelings for Lydia – "now he was in
love, for the first, the most
miraculous time."

*Lydia's benevolent ageing aunts,
Miss Juliana and Miss Bertie* (below),
are instrumental in arranging Lydia's
departure from her repressed,
obscure childhood and adolescence.
Juliana, "bony and large and
monolithic", appears at first to be
the assertive sister; but in fact it is
Bertie, who "had a sort of dampness
about her round soft face . . . that
made her seem self-effacing, without
power", who makes the important
decisions. Despite their fondness for
Richardson, they cannot influence
Lydia's feelings towards him.

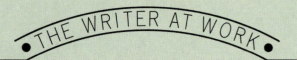

PAINTING WITH WORDS

Likened to a 'Renoir of the typewriter', H. E. Bates used words with the panache of a painter to shape and colour England's landscapes.

'I went off one evening and bought myself the thickest quarto writing pad, in pale blue, that I could find.' On this, the 17-year-old Bates wrote his first novel, a very substantial 150,000 words. A friend's reaction to the manuscript, and Bates' own cooler judgement, condemned it, and 'I buried the blue bundle of words away in a drawer, like a creature still-born.' This was by no means the last piece of writing that he discarded or destroyed. But unlike most aspiring authors, Bates had finished his novel, so confirming the strength and authenticity of his 'passionate, single-minded desire, to be a writer'.

Over the next 50 years he would publish hundreds of works of fiction, as well as a handful of plays, books on the English countryside, a study of the modern short story, and three volumes of autobiography full of insights into the writer's craft.

LITERARY MENTOR

Bates considered himself 'frigidly self-critical'. He also accepted, and learned by, the criticism of Edward Garnett, a publisher's reader whose past literary discoveries had included D. H. Lawrence, Joseph Conrad and John Galsworthy. After putting aside his first novel, Bates wrote a second, *The Two Sisters* (1926), which Garnett recommended his firm, Jonathan Cape, to accept. After a first meeting in which Bates was 'hypnotised and terrified by this enormous and grizzly figure', Garnett helped the unsophisti-cated young writer to place his work with London magazines, and became his severe but encouraging mentor. For years afterwards he admonished Bates for his *'facile side'*, but also told him, 'If you can write like this you need have no fear for the future.' The relationship was vital to Bates' artistic development, as he makes clear in his affectionate and respectful memoir of Garnett.

Over the next few years Bates established himself as a regional novelist, writing mainly about his native Nene Valley in books such as *The Fallow Land* and *The Poacher.* He made an even stronger reputation as a short-story writer. In this genre, Bates excelled through his mastery of precise and concentrated writing of the sort recommended by Edward Garnett. Bates spoke of the short story as his 'first love' and acknowledged that he had been influenced not only by older masters such as Chekhov, but also by the spare, direct,

The English countryside
(below) Revelling in descriptions of English country life, Bates drew on childhood memories where "every morning was golden".

Sir David Murray: The Heat of the Day/Fine Art Photographic Library

George Clausen: The Cart Horse/Fine Art Photographic

Harsh reality
The bleaker side of rural life (left) emerged in books such as The Fallow Land. *Nature was not always hospitable to the lonely farmer.*

The Photo Source

Russian masters
(right) Bates turned to writers such as Chekhov and Tolstoy (with white hat) for inspiration. But at times the 'inspiration' was too direct, and his editor, Edward Garnett, chastised Bates about a passage clearly plagiarized from Tolstoy.

pictorial style of his own contemporary, Ernest Hemingway.

Bates held that 'writing is just as much a graphic art as painting or drawing', and in his own work he aimed to depict 'scene and place and people vividly, in pictures, leaving out explanations, letting only essentials do the work'.

Although he was a passionate observer,

H. E. Bates believed that, for the writer of fiction, imagination was more important than facts: '. . . fiction is an exercise in the art of telling lies . . . The writer without imagination, or the ability to invent, is not a writer of fiction at all.' For a writer of this sort, a hint – rather than a history – sets the creative process working.

'The genesis of novels and stories . . .

often stems from the simplest, most fleeting of moments. A word, a glance, a face are, more often than not, enough'. *The Two Sisters* was suggested by a single event – a light glimpsed in the window of a strange, shadowy room. But the creative moment more often occurred when

Art and craft
Bates grew up amid "the distant pungent odours of leather and shoemakers' shops", and many of his fictional characters were based on urban craftsmen (below left). His own work was often done in his summer house (below).

Northampton Museum and Art Gallery

Popperfoto

His Action Station 1943 (detail) Poster designed by Tom Eckersley for the GPO/Imperial War Museum

pseudonym 'Flying Officer X' gave Bates his first great popular success. The tacit ban servicemen observed on talking about their deeds meant that Bates was drawing his inspiration from mere hints and clues. This admirably suited his talent for making great imaginative leaps from the smallest factual suggestion.

War, though it was a drain on his time, did nothing to dampen his creative imagination. Half of *Fair Stood the Wind for France,* the book that made him famous, was written in a fortnight, before a return to war work reduced him to finishing it in odd moments of leisure. The same working pattern arose on his visit to India and Burma, when he wrote *The Jacaranda Tree* (1949), *The Purple Plain* and *The Scarlet Sword.* 'Some of the white heat of Burma got into my blood as I wrote, so that the words came out as if driven by a blowtorch,' he recalled later.

MASTER OF THE NOVELLA

Eventually, Bates returned to the Nene Valley with *Love for Lydia.* It again sprang from a fusion of images – the sight of 'a strikingly beautiful young girl in a black cloak lined with scarlet', and a youthful visit to a local mansion, Rushden Hall. But it is also a rare autobiographical excursion into Bates' own adolescent feelings and impulses. His subsequent works were mainly novellas – short novels or long short stories – of which Bates became an acknowledged master. Works as varied and different as the Larkin books and *The Triple Echo* (1970) demonstrated that only death could still H. E. Bates' creative flow.

War heroics
Writing under the pseudonym 'Flying Officer X', Bates created some of his most popular stories about the exploits of World War II servicemen (above). A visit to Burma in 1945 (right) fired him "so that the words came out as if driven by a blowtorch."

Spectrum

Making movies
The film director David Lean (below, left) bought the rights to Fair Stood the Wind for France, The Cruise of the Breadwinner *and* The Purple Plain. *The admiration was mutual and Bates commented that "the story writer could learn much from the cinema."*

two unrelated experiences fused in Bates' mind. A junkheap which he passed on the edge of a bluebell wood and the sight of a vulgar family eating enormous ice creams meshed into *The Darling Buds of May.* His novel of the war in Burma, *The Purple Plain* (1947), was suggested by a 'single visit to a Burmese village and a post-demob conversation at Uxbridge in which an acquaintance casually mentioned a certain fighter pilot: "Remarkable type. Had more gongs than anyone I ever knew. And got them all for trying to kill himself."'

It was only during World War II, after 20 years of writing fiction, that H. E. Bates became a household name. Until then he had been forced to write rural-life journalism to make ends meet, and had never been paid as much as £10 for a short story. He had gained a commission in the RAF as a short-story writer, and ironically, the stories he wrote under the

Courtesy of Mrs H. E. Bates

WORKS·IN OUTLINE

One of the most prolific of modern writers, H. E. Bates is widely thought of as a novelist of English country life. Yet his novels and stories ranged over a vast variety of subjects, venturing into exotic locations and into every aspect of human emotions.

Charlotte's Row (1931) is set against a background of industrial squalor. *Fair Stood the Wind for*

France (1944) has often been called the best novel written about World War II. *The Scarlet Sword* (1950) draws on Bates' experiences in the East, while, in totally different vein, the bawdy, rumbustious Larkin family of *The Darling Buds of May* (1958) are brilliant comic creations. Spare and superb in its

craftsmanship, *The Triple Echo* (1970) is a late masterpiece.

Writer Henry Miller asserts, 'no matter how much one is made to suffer, one closes his books with a lasting sensation of beauty. And this sense of beauty . . . is evoked by the author's unswerving acceptance of life.' He also pays tribute to Bates' 'clean and healthy, and absolutely infectious' humour.

CHARLOTTE'S ROW

→ 1931 →

Masher Jonathan works in a brickyard (right) and lives with his shrill, avaricious, shopkeeper wife in Charlotte's Row, a street in a big industrial town. Among its other inhabitants is Masher's friend, Quintus Jabez Harper, "a healthy black-haired giant" of 50 who lords it over his family with a certain drunken grandeur. Nearby, a young boy, Adam, lives with his grandmother. Squalor and poverty oppress them all.

Despite his urban line of work, Masher has a deep love of the countryside, which he teaches in turn to Quintus' daughter Pauline, a factory worker. Eventually they run away together. The enraged Quintus assaults Masher's wife and goes to prison for it.

Meanwhile, Adam is sent out to work for a baker for a shilling a week, only to be brutally beaten for stealing a loaf. When Quintus leaves prison, he finds great changes have been wrought in his little domestic empire.

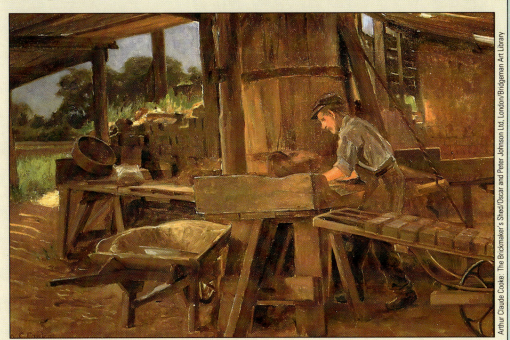

Arthur Claude Cooke : The Brickmaker's Shed/Oscar and Peter Johnson Ltd, London/Bridgeman Art Library

FAIR STOOD THE WIND FOR FRANCE

→ 1944 →

Returning from a bombing mission (left) John Franklin is forced to crash-land his Wellington bomber in occupied France. He is badly wounded, but his four-man crew carry him across country until they are taken in and given refuge by a girl who lives with her family in a quiet mill. Forged identity passes are obtained for the crew, who leave in pairs for England. But Franklin has to be left behind while his arm is amputated and he recuperates from the operation. The military situation in the locality becomes increasingly serious, with Germans taking and executing hostages. But Franklin and the girl, Françoise, have fallen in love. She decides to leave with him.

They cross to the relative safety of unoccupied (Vichy) France and make their way to Marseilles. There Franklin meets up again with one of his crew members, the erratic O'Connor. When the threesome try to reach Spain by rail, O'Connor's recklessness puts everything at risk . . .

ILN Picture Library

ILN Picture Library

THE SCARLET SWORD

◆ 1950 ◆

Set amid the turmoil and upheaval of the Partition of India (above), this is one of Bates' most exciting novels. Crane, a world-weary foreign correspondent, puts up at a Catholic mission in Kashmir. Here he meets Father Anstey and Father Simpson; McAlister, a Glaswegian nurse; an Indian 'dancer'; and two English families, the Mathiesons and the Maxteds. But the mission is soon overrun by Sikh and Hindu refugees, hotly pursued by ferocious Pathan tribesmen who storm the buildings. A night of terror follows before some kind of order is restored. The survivors remain in danger, however, both from the Pathans and from Indian planes which strafe the buildings day after day. Beset in this way, Crane inopportunely falls in love, Colonel Mathieson begins to crack, and Father Simpson displays unexpected qualities.

THE DARLING BUDS OF MAY

◆ 1958 ◆

This is the world's introduction to the Larkins (right) – sly, sharp Pop to whom everything is 'Perfick!', mountainous Ma 'almost two yards wide', and their six children. They live in amoral, overfed, rural bliss, complete with Rolls Royce and motor-boat thanks to Pop's junk dealing and other activities within the "black economy". Even the pregnancy of beautiful Mariette, who "hasn't made up her mind" about the father's identity, is accepted with equanimity. When Cedric Charlton, a proper young man from the Inland Revenue, visits in pursuance of his duty, he is effortlessly bamboozled, mesmerized by Mariette, and absorbed into the family. After hilarious adventures among the fruit-pickers and at a gymkhana in Pop's meadow, a marriage and a baby are imminent – but for whom?

Beryl Cook: The Darling Buds of May

70

SEVEN BY FIVE

→ 1963 ←

In a little hotel overlooking the sea (right), Harris and Madame Dupont meet, and an Anglo-French love affair blossoms despite the shadows of the recent war and the necessary deceptions of the present: *Across the Bay* is just one in this collection of 35 short stories representing 35 years of Bates' writing life (1926-61). The settings range from Tahiti, where, in *Mrs Eglantine,* the title character drinks her breakfast every morning at the hotel bar, to 'Evensford', the fictionalized version of Bates' birthplace and the setting used for *Lydia.*

In *The Enchantress*, Bertha, a girl from the Evensford slums, finds an easy path through life thanks to her chameleon-like adaptation to men's requirements. In other stories, a man emerges from long imprisonment for committing a crime of passion, only to blunder into a similar situation *(The Daffodil Sky);* and an 83-year-old ex-Indian Army colonel struggles to understand a group of young World War II flyers, wondering what has happened to one who has "bought it" (been killed) *(Colonel Julian).*

John MacLauchlan Milne: A Quayside in Normandy/Fine Art Photographic Library

THE TRIPLE ECHO

→ 1971 ←

The solitude of Alice Charlsworth is broken by Barton, a fair-haired, blue-eyed soldier stationed near her remote hill farm (left). Her husband is a prisoner-of-war of the Japanese, and 27-year-old Alice is left running the farm by herself. A chance encounter with Barton reveals him to be a farm boy at heart who hates the army. After he and Alice become lovers, he deserts.

Alice keeps him in seclusion in her house, passing him off as her sister when she has to explain the presence of another person on the farm. This disguise becomes increasingly convincing as Barton's hair grows longer and he adapts to his role with disconcerting completeness. Tension mounts when he attracts the amorous attentions of a local sergeant. To Alice's fury, he even agrees to go with the sergeant to a Christmas dance. Two days later the sergeant returns, this time in his role as a military policeman, intent on taking Barton away. But it is Alice who puts an unexpected end to this curious variation on the 'eternal triangle'.

ILN Picture Library

Industry's encroachment on the countryside, and the gradual disappearance of age-old farming techniques, transformed more than the landscape: it changed the nature of rural life.

Writing of his grandfather's Northamptonshire smallholding, outside Higham Ferrers, H. E. Bates recalled in *The Vanished World*, "it afforded me the foundation on which all the joys of childhood, together with all my feeling and love of the countryside is based".

as well as the sights of the countryside were transformed: "in the early days of this century England was a *quiet* country. There was no sound of lorries, cars, trains, aeroplanes or even tractors." The sounds of the countryside were the tink-tink of the blacksmith's forge, the clip-clop of horses'

22321   Rushden.   Old „Coach and Horses" Inn.

Days long gone
When Bates was a boy, the old Coach and Horses inn in Rushden (right) still served "small beer; which, though not strong enough for men, had body enough for boys or . . . 'bwoy-chaps'". But then the bwoy chaps of, say, 10 years old were already labouring half a day in school, half a day in the shoe factory and the evenings and weekends in the fields.

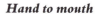

Hand to mouth
At the turn of the century, the seasonal cycle of farm work was done by manual labour (above) and horsepower (below). But as the population grew, old methods could not keep up with its needs.

By contrast, he dismissed nearby Rushden, the shoemaking town where he was born and bred, as a "mixture of blue slate, factory, chapel and that hard Midland red brick which equally oppressed heart, soul, eye and senses."

In Bates' novels real-life Rushden became the unsympathetically viewed town of Evensford. The narrator in *Love for Lydia* is clearly speaking with the author's own voice when he muses "Evensford . . . had taken the pattern of white hawthorn, the gold and the white, the dark steely brown of ploughed earth and the green of corn, and had left us ash-heaps." Bates could not forgive the destruction of the countryside by the encroaching industrial towns.

D. J. Watkins-Pitchford, better known as 'BB', the countryside author and illustrator, was born in 1905, the same year as H. E. Bates, and was also brought up in Northamptonshire. Like Bates he was acutely aware of the changes made to the countryside by the coming of chemical sprays, machinery and motor cars. The sounds and smells

Gilbert Spencer: A Cotswold Farm/Tate Gallery, London

James Bateman: Haytime in the Cotswolds/Southampton City Art Gallery

driven by the wheel's rotation, dispersed the seed.

Hand- and horse-power were the order of the day in Bates' youth. Threshing engines, however, might be at work in the rick yard and steam ploughing was catching on: "we imported on to that gut-lugging clay of ours two monsters in the shape of great steam engines, one stationed at one headland of a field, one at the other, the plough being drawn back and forth on a steel coil between." (*The Vanished World*). The last recorded instance of steam-tackle ploughing in Northamptonshire was as late as 1946.

BRINGING IN THE SHEAVES

The intractable five acres of heavy clay which Bates' grandfather farmed in the Nene Valley – land upon which horse after horse fell down dead, wearied from overwork – became the setting for *The Fallow Land*, published in 1932. Though times were hard and the work was unremitting, labour was in good supply and the fields were peopled with a lively cast of characters that were grist to a novelist's mill.

Shoemakers and other industrial workers from the towns worked in the harvest fields in the evenings and at weekends, joining "the great gangs of itinerant Irish labourers who had been seasonally invading England ever since Stuart times." Women and children peopled the harvest field too. After the corn was harvested they would glean the

Grandfather's horses
Bates recalls how his grandfather's farm horses, one by one, "fell down dead. Since their unremitting task was to draw plough, harrow, seed-drill, horse-hoe, trap and a truck . . . this was by no means surprising."

Mechanization was far beyond the means of such small-time farmers. The diesel-driven tractor was slow to catch on, though communally hired 'steam-tackle' was an increasingly familiar sight at ploughing time.

hooves, the barking of dogs and the bleating of sheep. When Bates was a boy, "the cornfield was flowery from end to end", before the use of chemical weed-killers 'ravaged' the countryside. Periwinkles, convolvulus, cowslips, corn-cockles, camomile, cornflower and poppies were abundant in the fields.

LIFE ON THE LAND

Despite the fertility of the land, the period from the late 1870s to 1939 was a time of great stagnation in British agriculture. Farming was in the doldrums (with only brief prosperity during World War I) and Northamptonshire's farmers were particularly badly hit. Between 1872 and 1929, for example, the country lost almost two-thirds of its arable acres as the recession bit deep.

During an era when transport had been revolutionized by the train, the car and the plane, and industry had become heavily mechanized, British agriculture had been left behind. Astonishing as it now seems, the horse was farming's main form of traction right up until 1939. Television and the atom bomb were just around the corner, but the bulk of British farmers had yet to reap the benefit of the petrol engine.

Although the horse-drawn seed drill had been around since the 1850s, in the early 1900s many farmers still walked the fields, broadcasting grain by hand. To sow grass seed the farmer might hand-push a broadcast barrow, which was essentially a long wooden seed hopper mounted on an iron wheelbarrow chassis. Revolving brushes,

Institute of Agricultural History and Museum of English Rural Life, University of Reading

Lost arts
Figures central to the 19th-century rural village, such as the smith (above) and the wheelwright (below), virtually disappeared with the coming of motor transport. Their skills were relegated to those of folk crafts, quaintly irrelevant to the fast-moving, mechanized world of the modern farm and village.

fallen corn from the stubble, descending on the "stook-empty fields like flocks of human hens, . . . gleaning frenziedly from dawn to dusk." The grain would produce flour enough to provide bread throughout the winter.

A favourite character of the young Bates was 'Smack'. "Shoemaker by day, he turned into pure peasant countryman by evening, beery, cunning, masterly with whet-stone and scythe." He turned up regularly to lend Bates' grandfather a hand at harvest time. Haymaking is thirsty work, and farmers brewed copious quantities of beer to keep their army of harvest workers happy. Smack, the scythesman, and his father apparently drank 25 pints a day in the hay-field or harvest-field.

The countryside provided a ready source of various kinds of home-brew. Country dwellers of Bates' 'Vanished World' were inveterate winemakers – cowslip and elderberry were great favourites – and Bates recalls that "Old women . . . were still brewing in my boyhood a herb beer, confined solely to summer, made of nettles, . . . dandelions, root ginger and various other wild hedgerow plants." Cottagers also made sloe-gin, as well as blackberry vinegar which was used as a throat-searing remedy for coughs.

HOOTERS AND HYMNS

Set amid the Nene Valley countryside which represented freedom for Bates, was the town of Rushden – a sort of prison. Its "factories, leather, chapels and factory hooters were a world we somehow had to escape from." Rushden, like many provincial towns caught up in the Industrial Revolution, had been a mere village of a few hundred people at the beginning of the 19th century. By the start of the 20th century it was a town of 15,000 people, centred around the shoemaking industry. The gas-lit, terraced streets were dreary, the "pattern of house, factory, bake-house and chapel, with here and there little front-room sweet shops, continued all over town." Children played their games on the street, disturbed occasionally by a bicycle, a tradesman's cart or a horse-drawn dray delivering leather.

Sundays in Rushden were dominated by Sunday School and numerous visits to the chapel, but they were relieved perhaps by the arrival of the water-cress man selling his produce in the streets or by

John Clayton Adams: Scything a Meadow/Fine Art photographic Library

Smoking short, nose-warming clay pipes, "they lived very largely on kippers, bloaters, tea, beer, cheese, potatoes and plenty of good bread from the coal-ovened bake-houses."

The independent hand-craftsmen worked long hours during the week, often "madly stitching and hammering away until midnight and even into the small hours in pursuit of cash." Come Saturday evening much of the money would be squandered in the pubs and there was a good deal of drunken brawling after hours.

By long tradition they did not go to work on Mondays but would head for the countryside to work on farms or go "rabbiting, coursing, mushrooming, following hounds, walking or riding miles by devious routes to secret hide-outs where bare-fisted bruisers bloodily battered themselves to pulp before crowds of gentry and poor alike."

BAD TIMES, GOOD TIMES

Times were changing in town as well as country. And the days of the hand-craftsman shoemaker, often working at home, were numbered, as machines and factories took over. One-trade towns like Rushden were severely hit in the 1920s by factory closures and short-time working. In *Love for Lydia* Evensford's "streets were melancholy with three-men bands of shuffling heroes with strips of medal ribbons pinned on narrow chests. Back doors were haunted by slow-footed men carrying suitcases . . . that opened to reveal meagre wardrobes of hanging shoelaces and cards of buttons and rolls of cheap pink and blue ribbon for threading through ladies' underwear."

Before the 1920s, entertainment of an organized kind was minimal. There were village fêtes and

Painful nostalgia
"The days in the hayfield were always hot, those in the harvest-field even hotter." But Bates' recollections of childhood summers ache with regret for the lost wild flowers, butterflies and birds which used to co-exist with the farmer's crop of hay (above) or grain. Chemical weedkillers and pesticides eradicated flora and fauna alike. A much greater loss was the wheat customarily gleaned by women and children (right) after hand-reaping and sheaving. With automation, far less grain was scattered. And some needy families had depended on gleanings for their winter bread.

the occasional country ramble. The tenor of weekdays was set by the shoe factories.

The shoemakers themselves were "shag-smoking, snuff-taking, stubble-faced working men, mufflered and capped" who visited the barber only on Wednesdays and Saturdays for a shave.

Institute of Agricultural History and Museum of English Rural Life, University of Reading.

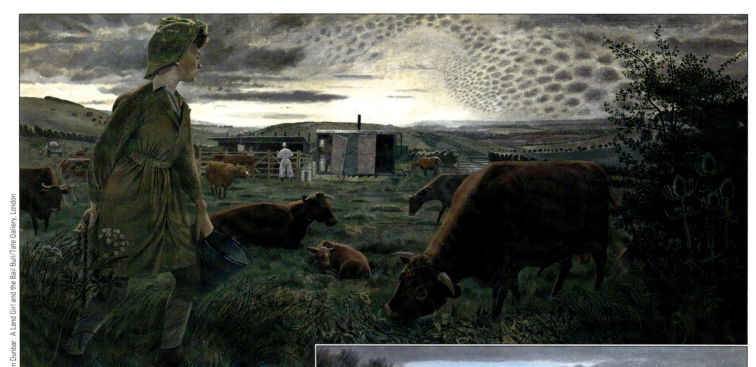

Evelyn Dunbar: A Land Girl and the Bail Bull/Tate Gallery, London

Vivian Pitchforth: Night Transport/Tate Gallery, London

chapel concerts, but the big day of the year, aside from Christmas, was Feast Sunday. Each of the Midlands' towns had their own, celebrated in July, August or September. "It was truly a business of feasting. It was an occasion for dressing-up, beer-swilling, parading the streets, family reunions, torchlight processions." The fair would come to town, with its "coconut shies, shooting galleries, hoop-las, helter-skelters, gingerbread, round-abouts and spit-rock."

By the 1920s there were shop-outings in charabancs and numerous dances at Parish and Co-op Halls, to which admission was one-and-six. If the dance was some distance away a group of friends might hire a private bus or, as in *Love for Lydia*, an ancient limousine taxi.

NOBLE ESTATES

Any opportunity of getting out of town gave Bates the sense of being let out of prison. It was on journeys by horse-drawn brake with his father's choir, as they travelled to perform at one of the great country houses, that he came to know some of the Halls which crop up so often in his fiction. The serenity and dignity of the noble estates was in marked contrast to the towns and differed also from the farming countryside.

Of the Sanatorium's grounds, in *Love for Lydia*, Richardson comments, "It was possible, up there, above the town . . . to feel, as at the Aspen house, that the town did not exist, that you were far away in clear, undesecrated country." Aspen house itself, of course, was based on Rushden Hall.

In *Spella Ho*, which was published in 1938 and became Bates' first American success, he traces the story of a Great House from 1873 to 1931 and of the uneducated, self-made man who vows to pos-

Sad necessities
The intensification of farming – specialization, mechanization, government intervention, the use of the Land Army in World War II (top) and the never-ending spread of road networks (above) all enhanced productivity. The days recalled so nostalgically by Bates were insecure, inefficient, grindingly hard labour by comparison. But his novels document the vanished beauty of this rural world with a wealth of loving detail.

sess it. The house is seen as a remnant of the old pastoral world standing out against the encroaching industrial world.

H. E. Bates' move to Kent in 1931 enabled him to see "with a clearer, far more objective vision the native Midland land I had left." With distance lending perspective, he wrote a spate of North-amptonshire novels – including *The Poacher* and *A House of Women* – with a keen awareness of the changes affecting the countryside he so loved. And the sights, sounds, smells and characters of Bates' youth proved to be a rich seedbed of inspiration and were vividly evoked time and again, most notably in *The Vanished World*. It is of that van-ished world, and particularly its countryside, that he writes so lyrically, capturing in painterly words an idyllic, halcyon period when "Always the air in June seems to have been clotted with the intoxication of mown grass, of may-blossom, of moon-daisies."

GRAHAM GREENE

← b.1904 →

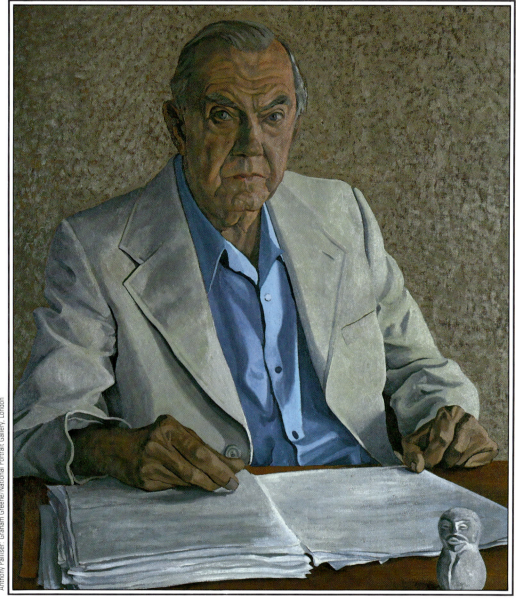

The most famous of living British novelists, Graham Greene
grips his millions of readers with dramatically conceived
narratives of the 20th-century world – a dangerous world in
which loyalties are uncertain and everything is at risk. Greene's
own life has been an eventful one. Above all, he has sought
relief from his inner tensions through two closely related 'ways
of escape' – writing and travelling – which have constantly
brought him on to 'the dangerous edge of things'.

COURTING DANGER

Jealous of his privacy and reticent about the contents of his long life, Graham Greene tells those who crave an insight into his nature and beliefs: 'Read my books.'

Much of Graham Greene's life remains firmly closed to the public. Although he shuns television appearances and journalistic interviews, he has written candidly enough about his early years; but his respect for 'the copyright of others' lives' – those closely involved with him – has made him doubly reticent to discuss any later events except those on public record. On the other hand, Greene has presented his own personality and motives in the starkest terms. He is prone to long, near-suicidal depressions and periods of intense boredom from which he can break loose only by taking extreme measures. Much of his life has been a search for 'ways of escape' – a phrase that he uses as the title of his second volume of autobiography. Among the 'ways' he numbers writing, travel and courting danger – activities in which his pronounced political and religious sympathies have been very much in evidence.

Henry Graham Greene was born on 2 October 1904 at Berkhamsted in Hertfordshire, where his father was a housemaster at the public (private) school. As one of six brothers and sisters, with six Greene cousins living only a few hundred yards away, he seems to have had a happy childhood – until at 13 he became a boarder at Berkhamsted School and 'the misery of life started'. The smells, the lack of privacy and the monotony appalled him, and since his father had by this time become headmaster, Greene found himself in a difficult position in relation to the other boys, who gave him his first experiences of betrayal and mental torture.

Over the years, Greene reacted to the horror of

A Variety of Lives: a biography of Sir Hugh Greene' by Michael Tracey, published by The Bodley Head Ltd.

The Greene clan
'The Greenes seemed to move as a tribe . . .' (Graham, aged 16, is pictured centre among relations).

Berkhamsted
'. . . a scene of happiness, misery, first love, the attempt to write.'

school life with successful truancies and occasional, inept attempts at self-destruction. Then, on the last day of the 1920 summer holidays, he took more positive action, leaving his parents a note to say that he would hide out on Berkhamsted Common until they agreed that he need not return to 'prison'. The outcome was anti-climactic, since Greene was found almost at once; but his gesture did persuade his parents that he was in distress, and they arranged for him to undergo psychoanalysis.

At the Lancaster Gate home of his analyst, Kenneth Richmond, Greene spent 'perhaps the happiest six months of my life'. The treatment may or may not have worked, but Greene now had two things he craved – freedom and access to the distractions of London. He returned to finish school at Berkhamsted, where, freed from most of the encumbrances of school life, he secured a place at Balliol College, Oxford, to study history. He was already writing 'the most sentimental fantasies in bad poetic prose', one of which, *The Tick of the Clock,* had appeared in his school magazine and was published in a London evening paper.

At Oxford, Greene wrote poetry, edited a magazine, the *Oxford Outlook,* and began his long interest in the cinema. He and his friend Claude Cockburn became members of the Communist Party for a few weeks – mainly, Greene says,

'Memories' Collectors Shop, London

Courtesy of Berkhamsted School

Charles Henry Greene
As headmaster of Berkhamsted School (above right) Graham's father (above) 'was even more distant than our aloof mother'.

Key Dates

1904 born in Berkhamsted

1920 psychoanalysed

1922 Balliol College, Oxford

1926 converts to Catholicism; sub-editor on *The Times*

1927 marries Vivien Dayrell-Browning

1929 publishes first novel

1938 *Brighton Rock;* visits Mexico

1941 intelligence work in Sierra Leone

1943 intelligence work in London

1950s travels in Malaya, Vietnam, Cuba, Kenya, Congo, etc.

1960s travels in Haiti, Chile, Paraguay

1966 settles in Antibes; *The Comedians*

Propaganda aid
Greene wrote for the Germans – and got £25 and a trip to Trier (right) in 1924 for his efforts.

Zefa Picture Library

because they hoped it might get them a free holiday to Moscow. One absurd result of this was that for many years – even after he became famous as a 'Catholic novelist' – Greene was allowed only a restricted right of entry to the United States. A more rewarding involvement with politics began when Greene offered his services as a propagandist to the Germans of the Ruhr, who were then – after World War I – suffering under French occupation. This brought him a free holiday down the Rhine and Moselle valleys as an 'observer'. Mysterious visitors continued to frequent his Oxford rooms for some time, but his plans for adopting the role of a double agent were thwarted when the Ruhr problem was solved by international agreement.

DEATH WISH

In spite of such diversions, Greene's Oxford years gave rise to a crisis that reveals a great deal about him. During the long vacation of 1923 he fell obsessively in love with the governess of the youngest Greenes. His lack of success with her

evidently contributed to a chronic attack of 'ennui' which persisted until Greene looked in a cupboard and found a revolver belonging to his elder brother – 'a small ladylike object with six chambers'. Having read about Russian roulette, he decided to take the risk on Berkhamsted Common. He put a bullet in one of the chambers, spun the chambers round, then put the revolver to his head and pulled the trigger, knowing that there was a one in six chance of killing himself. Having survived, Greene felt an extraordinary sense of jubilation and a conviction that 'life contained an infinite number of possibilities'. After several more 'games', Russian roulette lost its thrill, but Greene's discovery of danger as a stimulant was to be a permanent influence on his outlook.

After Oxford, Greene was briefly a trainee with the British-American Tobacco Company, worked as a tutor (becoming so bored that he had a perfectly good tooth extracted in order to enjoy a 'holiday' under ether), and secured an unpaid job with *The Nottingham Journal*.

Having become engaged to a Roman Catholic, he felt that he should know something of her beliefs, received instruction, and unexpectedly found himself convinced by the priest's arguments. He was received into the Church in February 1926 – the beginning of a complex, problematical relationship that has now lasted for over 60 years.

A FALSE START

In March 1926 Greene was accepted as a sub-editor on *The Times*, where his job was to condense and remodel the news stories sent in by reporters. Thanks to this secure and highly respectable employment he was able to marry Vivien Dayrell-Browning in 1927, eventually becoming the father of two children. Meanwhile he had written two novels that were refused publication, and had begun a third, *The Man Within*, while in hospital with appendicitis. When *The Man Within* was accepted, published in 1929, and sold some 8,000 copies, Greene became convinced that he would be able to live as a professional writer. He

Hutchison Library

The Times

No. 44263.   London Wednesday May 5, 1926   Price 2d.

WEATHER FORECAST. Wind N.E.; fair to dull; risk of local rain.

THE GENERAL STRIKE.

A wide response was made yesterday throughout the country to the call of those Unions which had been ordered by the T.U.C. to bring out their members. Railway workers stopped generally, though at Hull railway clerks are reported to have resumed ordinary work, confining themselves to their ordinary work, and protested against the strike. Commercial road transport was only partially suspended. In London the tramways and the L.G.O.C. services were stopped. The printing industry is practically at a standstill, but lithographers have not been withdrawn, and compositors in London have not received instructions to strike. Large numbers of building operatives, other than those working on housing, came out.

The situation in the engineering trades was confused; men in some districts stopped while in others they continued at work. There was no interference with new construction in the shipbuilding yards, but in one or two districts some of the men engaged on repair work joined in the strike with the dockers.

Food.—Supplies of milk and fish brought into Kings Cross, Euston and Paddington were successfully distributed from the Hyde Park Depot and stations. The Milk & Food Controller expects it will be possible to maintain a satisfactory supply of milk to hospitals, institutions, schools, hotels, restaurants and private consumers. Milk will be 6d. per gallon dearer wholesale and 2d. per quart retail to-day. Smithfield market has distributed 5,000 tons of meat since Monday.

Mails:—Efforts will be made to forward by means of road transport the mails already shown as due to be dispatched very shortly from London. The position is uncertain and the f... be limited to m... Africa. ...t Bow Stre... ...required

Liverpool, Leeds, Northampton, Cardiff, Portsmouth, Dover, N.Derbyshire and Monmouthshire.

Evening papers appeared at Bristol, Southampton, several Lancashire towns and Edinburgh, and typescript issues at Manchester, Birmingham and Aberdeen.

The Atlantic Fleet did not sail on its summer cruise at Portsmouth yesterday. The men went on shore duty.

Road & Rail Transport:—There was no railway passenger transport in London yesterday except a few suburban trains. Every available form of private transport was used. A few independent omnibuses were running, but by the evening the railway companies, except the District and Tubes, had an improvised service. Among the railway services to-day will be:— 9.30 a.m. Manchester to Marylebone; 9.30 a.m. Marylebone to Manchester; 10.10 a.m Marylebone to Newcastle; 9 a.m. Norwich to London; 9 a.m King's Cross to York; 5 p.m. King's Cross to Peterborough; 9 p.m. Peterborough to King's Cross. L.M.S. Electric trains between Watford and Euston and Broad Street will maintain a 40 minutes service. On all sections of the Metropolitan Railway except Moorgate to Finsbury Park, a good service will run to-day from 6.40 a.m. The Underground hope to work a six minute service on the Central London Line to-day from 8 a.m. to 8 p.m. between Wood Lane and Liverpool Street. The following stations only will be open:— Shepherds Bush, Lancaster Gate, Oxford Circus, Tottenham Court Road, Bank, Liverpool Street. A flat fare of 3d will be charged.

The Prime Minister had an audience of the King yesterday morning

There was no indication last night of any attempt to resume negotiations ...ma... have to ...tween the Pri... Minister and the ...rinting en... India &... The Go... who newspap... will... de... die...

British Library

persuaded his publishers to pay him £200 a year for three years and, against all advice, resigned from *The Times*.

'I left *The Times* the author of a successful first novel. I thought I was a writer already and that the world was at my feet, but life wasn't like that. It was only a false start.' Greene took his family to Chipping Campden in the Cotswolds, where they could live cheaply while he established himself. Instead, he produced two novels that failed commercially and were, in Greene's view, so bad that he has never allowed them to be reprinted. A third, *Stamboul Train,* was to be much more successful, although expensive changes had to be made to the text when the novelist J. B. Priestley threatened to sue for libel.

LONG ROUTE TO *BRIGHTON*

For most of the 1930s, Greene was in debt to his publishers, and could not support his family by his fiction. He survived by writing and reviewing for the *Spectator* and *Night and Day,* among other things contributing regular film criticism for four and a half years. Here too he fell foul of the libel laws (then more stringent than they are today) when he suggested that the child star Shirley Temple 'had a certain adroit coquetry which appealed to middle-aged men'. He was also able to earn some much-needed money by writing film scripts for the producer Alexander Korda, although the results were uninspiring. His film work did not take off until after the war, when Greene wrote *The Fallen Idol* and *The Third Man.*

Greene had already discovered the lure of travel as a 'way of escape'. His most ambitious — and

Defending The Times
In the 1926 General Strike, Greene uncharacteristically pitted himself against the strikers who had, after all, set fire to the building. 'I was emotionally attached to the newspaper' (left).

Journey without mishap
A three-months' trip in 1935 through Liberia (right), walking 15 miles a day, resulted in the book Journey Without Maps. *It was immediately suppressed.*

hazardous — pre-war journey was a trip through Liberia and Sierra Leone, made with his 23-year old cousin Barbara. No detailed map of the area existed, and the travellers made do with an American military map that labelled large blank areas with the single word 'cannibals'. The travel book that was to justify the expedition (*Journey Without Maps,* 1936) was suppressed after another threat of a libel action, but Greene managed to clear his debt to his publishers when his first major novel, *Brighton Rock* (1938), enjoyed some success. The same year he visited Mexico, where the Church was being persecuted — an experience which inspired *The Lawless Roads* and his famous novel, *The Power and the Glory.*

Greene also tried, unsuccessfully, to visit Spain during the Civil War in which his sympathies were strongly anti-fascist. The political crises of the 1930s gave him a further motive for travel: 'A restlessness set in then which has never quite been allayed: a desire to be a spectator of history.' But when it became apparent that Britain herself would soon be engulfed by war, Greene raced to make some provision for his family, writing a thriller, *The Confidential Agent,* in six weeks in the mornings (with the help of benzedrine), while going on more slowly in the afternoons with *The Power and the Glory.*

During World War II, Greene's life took on some of the qualities of his fiction. He worked at the Ministry of Information during the Blitz before being recruited into MI6 by his sister Elizabeth. He was sent to West Africa and, after

Phil Selfe/Zefa Picture Library

Sierra Leone
Posted to Freetown (above), from 1942 to 1943 Greene ran a one-man SIS office — inspiration for The Heart of the Matter.

A reckless move
Throwing up his job with The Times, *Greene moved, with his family, to Chipping Campden (left), bent on being a full-time author. Poverty struck.*

Liba Taylor/Hutchison Library

Mexican journey
Travelling through the Chiapas mountains (above), Greene was deeply shocked by his first-hand experience of suppression of religion.

three months' training at Lagos (Nigeria), went on to Freetown (Sierra Leone) – supposedly as a member of Special Branch CID – where he established a one-man office. He has dismissed his activities there as 'futile efforts to run agents into the Vichy colonies'. In 1943 Greene returned to London and was given responsibility for counter-espionage in Portugal. He worked under Kim Philby, who became a friend; Philby's own secret career, as a Soviet agent, still had a good many years to run before exposure.

It was only after the war that Greene, then in his forties, became a famous and popular writer. *The Heart of the Matter* (1948), a book he now dislikes, was 'the start of my success', and the film *The Third Man* became a box-office hit. From this time

DOUBLE AGENT

The Keystone Collection

During World War II, Greene worked for British Intelligence. His superior was Kim Philby (right). In 1951 two British diplomats, Guy Burgess and Donald Maclean, were identified as long-term Soviet agents, but managed to defect before they could be arrested. Clearly they had been tipped off. The insider – the 'third man' – proved to be Kim Philby, who finally disappeared in the Middle East to re-emerge in Moscow as a KGB officer. Greene admired Philby's secret dedication to a cause throughout his long double life: 'Philby really lived out his loyalty.' And when Greene came to write a novel about a double agent (*The Human Factor*), he sent it to Philby for expert comment.

The quiet observer
Four times Greene went
to Indo-China (above), once
taking tea with Ho Chi
Minh in Hanoi. In 1955,
he sympathized with both
factions in North Vietnam.

The Keystone Collection

onwards, each new Graham Greene novel was an important public event, and the writer's opinions carried increasing weight. His insight into dilemmas of conscience and motive caused him to be consulted by numerous fellow-Catholics, so that he felt himself 'used and exhausted by the victims of religion'.

Ironically, Greene's own religious position had become problematic. By the 1950s he had ceased to be a communicant because his private life was 'not regular', although he continued to express his often unorthodox views on Catholic matters. More recently he has ruefully described himself as 'semi-lapsed' but with 'one foot in the door'.

THE HABIT OF DANGER

For Greene the 1950s were 'a period of great unrest', and he travelled more widely than ever. Characteristically he explains that 'it became a habit with me to visit troubled places, not to seek material for novels but to regain the sense of insecurity which I had enjoyed in the three blitzes on London.' Often undertaking journalistic assignments, he spent long periods in Malaya during the Emergency, in Vietnam while the French fought the Viet Minh, in Kenya when the Mau Mau were killing white farmers, and also in Stalinist Poland, pre-Castro Cuba and the Belgian Congo. Although some of his most famous novels emerged from these experiences, Greene also found an escape from the solitude of the fiction writer by beginning a new career as a successful playwright.

He greatly relished his involvement in rehearsing and mounting theatrical productions.

In 1966 Greene finally left England and settled at Antibes in the South of France. But despite advancing age he remained an indefatigable traveller, still attracted by novelty and danger, and moved to join the struggle against oppression.

'One of my commitments'
A picture hangs on Greene's wall, a gift from Fidel Castro (above). 'I felt very close to the Fidelistas' struggle.'

Fact or Fiction

ALEXANDER KORDA

The only character Greene admits to taking from life is Dreuther, the business tycoon in *Loser Takes All*, modelled on Greene's film-producer friend Alex Korda (right). The expansive Hungarian also gave Greene the plot, by failing to show up at a rendezvous for a Mediterranean cruise, just as Dreuther does – though, unlike his fictional counterpart, Greene did not find consolation by winning a fortune at roulette.

Popperfoto

General Torrijos
The left-wing ruler of Panama (above) invited Greene to visit in 1974 and regularly afterwards; they became close friends. 'I fell in love with Panama and its people, just like that, without warning . . . Torrijos knew that I was inclined to take an anti-American attitude.'

Sandinistas in buying bullets which, I hoped, would eventually hit Somoza' (the dictator of Nicaragua, who was eventually overthrown). Of course, as is said in *The Comedians*, "A pen, as well as a silver bullet, can draw blood."

While involved in all these activities, Greene continued to produce books, albeit more slowly than in earlier years. He has not left the South of France untouched by his pen (in 1982 he published a pamphlet with the title *J'Accuse – The Dark Side of Nice*). But danger has not sought out Graham Greene, and it seems that he is spending the later 1980s there without recourse to 'ways of escape'.

Sandinista sympathizer
The Sandinistas in Nicaragua (above) 'asked me to join them as an observer; I refused: Somoza could have had me shot down and put the blame on my friends . . .' Greene (below) feels fame now both frees and hampers him as a political activist.

Some of his actions have been public gestures, given added authority by his ever-growing fame: a protest in Prague against repression in Czechoslovakia; resignation from the American Academy of Letters during the Vietnam war; condemnation of British methods of interrogating IRA suspects. But Greene has also enjoyed taking a hand in events – carrying a message to Ho Chi Minh, smuggling winter clothing to Castro's rebel followers, meeting Haitian rebels . . . and, apparently in a spirit closer to mischief than to militancy, getting himself deported from Puerto Rico by the Americans, and talking to schoolchildren in right-wing Paraguay on the forbidden subject of Fidel Castro.

BUYING BULLETS

In his seventies Greene became involved with the left-wing ruler of Panama, General Torrijos, whom he supported in Panama's dispute with the United States over the canal. When the matter was resolved in 1977, Greene went to Washington as part of the Panamanian delegation, thoroughly enjoying the irony of his official status in a country which had once been reluctant to grant him entry. More recently still, he was 'a modest help to the

THE COMEDIANS

Overshadowed by the dark and violent menace of a brutal regime, a group of foreigners react according to their beliefs. The most fortunate have passionate commitments; others long to care.

Set in Haiti at the beginning of 'Papa Doc' Duvalier's reign of terror, *The Comedians* is a story about the committed and the uncommitted. An odd collection of characters makes its way to the island on board a Dutch cargo-ship. Victims of whim and circumstance, they are 'comedians' in the face of appalling tragedy and brutality. Economical and beautifully written, the novel is a compelling read. Greene uses humour and irony with great skill in his treatment of very serious issues.

GUIDE TO THE PLOT

The main characters meet on board the *Medea* bound for Haiti. Brown, the narrator, has failed to sell his Haitian luxury hotel in the United States and is returning for want of something better to do. The Smiths, with their absurd mission of establishing a vegetarian centre in the poverty-stricken island, arouse Brown's exasperation and sympathy. He invites them to stay at his hotel – his first guests for a long time. The mysterious Jones, who insists on calling himself Major, is full of tales and hints at his own dark past.

On his first evening back in Haiti, Brown renews his affair with Martha Pineda, the German wife of a South American Ambassador. They soon quar-

> "'Vegetarianism isn't only a question of diet, Mr Brown. It touches life at many points. If we really eliminated acidity from the human body we would eliminate passion.'
>
> 'Then the world would stop.'
>
> He reproved me gently, 'I didn't say love,' and I felt a curious sense of shame."

rel and Brown realizes that nothing has changed in his absence. He loves her, but is unbelievably jealous, painfully aware that she might deceive him, just as she is deceiving her husband. He is also resentful of her spoilt son Angel, who has a stranglehold on his mother's affections and has to be bribed with sweets.

The island's troubles are getting worse. The curfew has been lifted, but the streets of Port-au-Prince are filled with fear. The Tontons Macoutes, Duvalier's secret police, and their road blocks are everywhere. Brown's first problem when he reaches his vacant, decaying hotel is to dispose of the body of the ex-Minister for Social Welfare, which lies curled up in the

Luxury hotel
Brown returns to Haiti having failed to sell his hotel. His loyal barman Joseph stayed, despite torture by the Tontons Macoutes.

Paul Hogarth ©1996. Grand Hotel Oloffson, Port-au-Prince, Haiti, from 'Graham Greene Country' published by Pavilion Books

empty swimming pool. Suddenly out of favour with the President, the Minister had to escape torture and chose Brown's hotel in which to commit suicide.

Later, at the Pinedas' for drinks one evening, Brown meets Philipot junior, the dead minister's nephew. His uncle's death convinces Philipot of the need for armed insurrection. Young and idealistic, he imagines a single Bren gun would be enough to destroy Duvalier. During the evening, Brown is desperate for Martha. Certain that her husband knows about their affair, he tries to make love to Martha upstairs, as if to claim her as his own in her husband's house.

Meanwhile Jones has formed connections in high places and is seen, at Mère Catherine's brothel, in the company of Captain Concasseur, a powerful Tontons Macoutes leader. It is clear that Jones has a grand scheme for making a fortune, but before he can tie up loose ends, Concasseur becomes suspicious, and Jones, in fantastic disguise, aided by Brown and the Medea's Dutch captain, is forced to seek refuge in the Pinedas' embassy. Brown, spurred on by the Marxist doctor Magiot, later risks his own life when he delivers Jones to Philipot junior and the rebels in the mountains, although his motivation is selfish rather than political or humanitarian. Jones finally gets the chance to prove himself and to earn Brown's respect with his courage.

HUMAN POTENTIAL

The Comedians is a satirical novel that explores with great subtlety the life of those who never fully engage with their reality. The story exposes the futility of living on the edge of human experience where lack of commitment and passion leads to a dissatisfied restlessness. The gentle, mocking tone of much of the novel belies the seriousness of its concerns. Many of the characters are shown to be in some way absurd, and yet also to possess admirable qualities, as if to illustrate the unlimited potential of human beings to contribute something of value to the world. In contrast, Duvalier and his henchmen are testimony to the unfathomable depravity to which human beings can descend.

Faced with a dictatorship based on brutality and corruption, the characters in the story behave in very different ways. The 'comedians' of the story are the ones who pretend to be something they are not, and who find themselves, in this case, trapped in a nightmare. All expatriates with western concepts of democracy, they can barely believe in the terror

MGM/Kobal Collection

Vegetarians unite
A world free of acidity through vegetarianism is what the Smiths (above) aim to promote in Haiti.

Passion and mistrust
Unable to believe in anyone, Brown renews his uneasy affair with Martha (below).

Devil or Angel?
Martha's son (right) jealously watches her every step. She and Brown meet furtively, making love in a car, next to a statue in the harbour (below).

MGM/National Film Institute, London

Paul Hogarth ©1986: Henri Christophe statue, Port-au-Prince, Haiti, from 'Graham Greene Country' published by Pavilion Books

MGM/National Film Institute, London

85

Reader's Guide

Duvalier has brought to the island. The ambassador Pineda wonders whether even Papa Doc himself is perhaps a comedian. It is Philipot, the Haitian revolutionary, who corrects him: "Oh no . . . he is real. Horror is always real."

Brown is an archetypal outsider, of uncertain parentage, forced to live on his wits to make a living, whose only philosophy is to "take things as they come". He ends up in Haiti by sheer coincidence and stays simply because he has nowhere else to go. A few years of success with the hotel, followed by a total collapse of the island's tourist industry, serve only to confirm his ironic belief that life is after all a comedy, not a tragedy. Educated by Jesuits to have faith in the Christian God as "incarnated in every tragedy", Brown comes to believe in God as an "authoritative practical joker . . . there must be a power which always arranges things to happen in the most humiliating circumstances".

CITIZEN OF NOWHERE

Brown is a cynic; but above all it is his sense of not belonging to anyone or anywhere that keeps him dispassionate. He has no emotional connections with

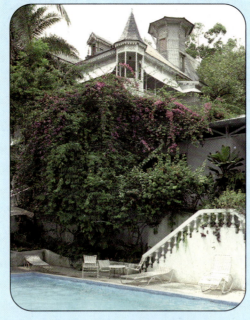

Patricia Booth/Camera Press, London

The empty pool
The hotel's swimming pool (above) – once a focal point for tourists – is now haunted by the memory of the ex-minister Philipot who committed suicide in it.

Held in custody
Major Jones (below centre) is arrested soon after arriving. But he befriends the Tontons, due more to his own cunning than to Brown or Smith's intervention.

Monte Carlo, his birthplace. Instead he feels a greater tie to Haiti:

"... here, in the shabby land of terror, chosen for me by chance . . . transience was my pigmentation; my roots would never go deep enough anywhere to make me a home or make me secure with love."

Instead Brown inhabits the lonely half-world of his empty hotel and conducts his illicit love affair in the back seat of a car. His life is barren and he is forced to invent a missing reality. His lover Martha accuses him of living in a fictional world:

"You should have been a novelist . . . then we would all have been your characters. We couldn't say to you we are not like that at all, we couldn't answer back . . . don't you see you are inventing us?"

> "Even while I made love to her I tested her. Surely she wouldn't have the nerve to take me if she were expecting another man at the rendezvous, and then I told myself that it wasn't a fair test – she had nerve for anything."

MGM/Kobal Collection

Sarah Errington/Hutchison Library

exaggerated belief in the essential good-ness of people, especially black people, have a faith in their mission and in each other which shines through the corrup-tion and apathy of those around them.

Brown and Martha, in comparison, are observers of a world that exists apart from them. They make love to the sound of guns and terror, and remain somehow unaffected. Martha envies Magiot his

Road to Duvalierville
(left) Road-blocks halt traffic on the road north, "along which, as most people . . . hoped, the tanks would one day come".

In the mountains
Philipot Junior has joined the rebels. Subsequently, Brown delivers Major Jones to their mountain camp to lead the guerillas.

MGM/National Film Institute, London

Stuck in Haiti, he imagines the tourists may yet return, and in the meantime uses the unhappy drama of his affair with Martha to justify why he must stay. He can tolerate the dreadful regime in the same way he can tolerate anything: "Perhaps there is an advantage in being born . . . without roots, for one accepts more easily what comes."

The characters in the novel who have

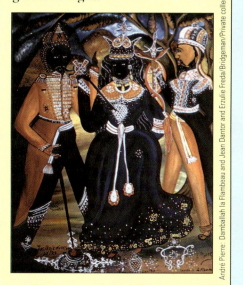
some sense of belief or commitment to an ideal, stand in contrast to Brown. Doctor Magiot especially, with his calm, quiet courage, makes a determined stand against the Duvalier dictatorship because he believes in something better. He knows his efforts as a communist will be ineffectual: he understands the Americans would never allow Haiti to go the way of Cuba. And yet his faith in a kinder, more humane and equal future makes him a heroic figure.

According to Doctor Magiot, Brown's mother was another believer. Committed to living life to the full, she would have been up in the mountains with the rebels, unlike her son, whose seeming indifference to Haiti's troubles profoundly disturbs Magiot. Even the Smiths, with their

communism and her husband and Brown their Catholicism. It is as if her lack of belief in anything makes it impossible for her to love. Brown recognizes that:

"Neither of us would ever die for love. We would grieve and separate and find another. We belonged to the world of comedy and not of tragedy."

Greene does not suggest in the novel that those who have a commitment to life make any real difference to the course of events. The Smiths are unlikely to estab-lish their vegetarian centre in Haiti, and the rebels will probably die. Life is, after all, a 'confused comedy'. But the essential difference lies within: Magiot and the Smiths have a faith that gives them a reason to live. Brown has nothing, except his empty hotel.

CHARACTERS IN FOCUS

The people in *The Comedians* are striking in how different they are from one another. It would be hard to imagine a more varied mixture than the passengers on board *The Medea* bound for one of the world's worst trouble spots. The different ways they each react to the crisis in Haiti illustrate the main concern of the novel: life is absurdly unpredictable. The only real way to bring meaning to the madness is to believe in something bigger than yourself. Consequently Doctor Magiot and the Smiths, with their commitment to creating a better world, fare better than the rootless Brown and Jones.

WHO'S WHO

Mr Brown	The cynical and mistrustful narrator who belongs nowhere and dreams of former carefree days.
Major Jones	"A small man, very tidily dressed . . . he certainly did not mean to be conspicuous."
Mr and Mrs Smith	The somewhat comic vegetarian missionaries who see only the best in human nature.
Martha Pineda	Independent and honest, she is unhappy both in her marriage and in her affair with Brown.
Angel Pineda	Martha's son, "he was too fat for his age, he had his father's eyes like brown buttons, he sucked bonbons, he noticed things, and he made claims."
Mr Pineda	Martha's husband, he is very possessive: "I have never heard a man use the word 'my' more frequently."
Comtesse de Lascot-Villiers	Brown's flamboyant mother whose commitment to living life to the full earns her much respect.
Doctor Magiot	Brown's advisor, friend and guide, the Marxist doctor "was very big and very black, but he possessed great gentleness".
Joseph	The hotel's limping barman who stays on as a loyal dogsbody.

Roger Coleman

The central character in the story, Brown (above) is also the ultimate outsider. He returns to his empty hotel, long after the tourists have gone; he has lost his Catholic faith; he lacks Magiot's political convictions; he cannot even trust his mistress. He had "left involvement behind me . . . I had felt myself not merely incapable of love . . . but even of guilt."

Major Jones (right) is the real 'comedian' of the novel, weaving a web of half-lies about his experiences in Burma and the Congo to impress. He divides the world into natural winners ('toffs') and hangers-on ('tarts'): "The toffs can do without the tarts, but the tarts can't do without the toffs. I'm a tart."

Vegetarians with a mission, Mr and Mrs Smith (right) saw their moment of glory back in '48 when Mr Smith ran as a presidential candidate, polling 10,000 votes. They are convinced that a vegetarian diet will bring out the innate goodness in everyone, but their patronizing naivety lands them in difficult situations. They show great tenacity and strength of purpose, however, and Mrs Smith in particular wins Brown's admiration. "I had many quarrels with her in the course of time, she suspected that I laughed a little at her husband, but she never knew how I envied them. I have never known in Europe a married couple with that kind of loyalty."

Bored and frustrated as the wife of a diplomat, Martha Pineda (left) lives her life primarily for her son Angel and for her hopelessly unhappy liaison with the cynical Mr Brown. "Many months later when the affair was over", Brown comments, "I realized and appreciated her directness. She played no part. She answered exactly what I asked. She never claimed to like a thing that she disliked or to love something to which she was indifferent."

"I could understand why it was these men wore dark glasses [below] – they were human, but they mustn't show fear: it might be the end of terror in others." The plain-clothes, strong-arm Tontons Macoutes who enforce the corrupt Haitian regime intimidate, torment, torture and humiliate routinely. "There was no hurry; they were secure; they were the law." The Haitians invest them with the mystical wickedness of 'zombies' and voodoo.

Roger Coleman

THE HUMAN FACTOR

Although his plots may tackle social evils and repression, Greene always focuses on individuals – their absurdity, their conscience, their feeble aspirations to glory, their powerlessness.

A favourite quotation from the Victorian poet Robert Browning – 'Our interest's on the dangerous edge of things' – has been cited by Graham Greene as an entirely appropriate description of his work; and the same poem identifies such typical Greene characters as 'the honest thief, the tender murderer, the superstitious atheist'. As these lines suggest, Greene's fictional world is a desperately insecure place, peopled by divided or ambiguous characters who may at any moment find themselves betrayed, whether by others or by their own natures. It is a world of violence and dramatic developments. More than any other modern master, Greene is as concerned with action as with character, casting works of the highest seriousness in the form of thrillers (often pursuit stories), in a manner that has brought him enormous popularity. And even before his long connection with films and filming began, Greene's work had a dynamic, essentially cinematic quality because, 'When I describe a scene, I capture it with the moving eye of the cine-camera rather than with the photographer's eye – which leaves it frozen.'

ENTERTAINMENT AND 'WORTH'

Down to 1958 Greene divided his works into 'novels' and 'entertainments'. The entertainments included books such as *Stamboul Train* (1932), *A Gun for Sale* (1936) and *The Confidential Agent* (1939), in which the thriller element took prece-dence. There was relatively little character development – although 'the dangerous edge of things' loomed large in such narratives, which mirrored with unromantic accuracy a world in which secret police and political assassinations were becoming the norm.

The distinction between Greene's novels and his entertainments seemed particularly relevant when he began to be recognized as an outstanding 'Catholic novelist' with the publication of *Brighton Rock* (1938), *The Power and the Glory* (1940), *The Heart of the Matter* (1948) and *The End of the Affair* (1951). Greene himself has always objected to being called a Catholic novelist ('detestable term!'), insisting that he is simply a novelist who happens to be a Catholic. It is certainly true that Greene's narratives are far from

Twentieth Century-Fox/National Film Institute, London

A bad press
While reviewing for the young magazine Night and Day, *Greene invited the wrath of the 9-year-old Shirley Temple and film-makers Twentieth Century-Fox for libelling the film* Wee Willie Winkie *(above). The court action contributed to the early eclipse of* Night and Day.

'A book to please'
'I'd got a baby coming, only about £20 in the bank . . . so I thought I really must get on with it.' Stamboul Train *(1932) (left) was Greene's first and only attempt to write a purely entertaining, commercial book. Because Greene could only afford a train ticket as far as Cologne, the background descriptions become more vague as the train travels south.*

being simplistic pious fables, and the conclusions that readers draw from them tend to be of dubious orthodoxy – so much so that *The Power and the Glory* was actually condemned by the Holy Office. Furthermore Greene's Catholic characters live even more precariously 'on the dangerous edge of things' than the others, since for them the stakes are higher: they risk not only destruction but damnation. Rose in *Brighton Rock* prefers to be damned with Pinkie rather than saved on her own, while Scobie in *The Heart of the Matter* pities and tries to spare others even as he plans the mortal sin of suicide. Catholicism too is part of Greene's thriller-like vision of life.

Whether or not Greene should properly be described as a Catholic novelist, his

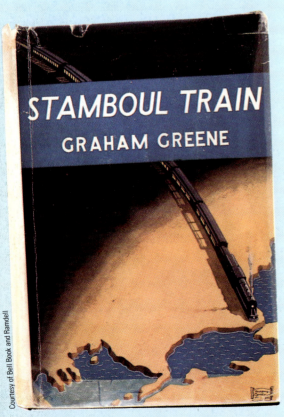

Courtesy of Bell Book and Ramdell

STAMBOUL TRAIN
GRAHAM GREENE

four famous novels of 1938-51 are undoubtedly concerned with 'the appalling strangeness of the mercy of God'. But they represent a relatively brief phase in his career: since 1951 specifically religious issues have not dominated his works, although faith and unbelief, commitment and indifference remain his central concerns. Travel has continued to supply not only settings for novels (although in travelling 'I wasn't seeking sources, I stumbled on them'), but also legitimate occasions for the portrayal of violence and insecurity – war in Vietnam (*The Quiet American*, 1955), Cuba before Castro (*Our*

The Keystone Collection

'The Living Room'
Greene is pictured right with the stars of his 1953 hit play – Eric Portman and an 'unknown' Dorothy Tutin.

Brian Moser/Hutchison Library

Religious awe
Simple, fervent 'primitive' Catholicism (left) convinced Greene true religion was 'the peasant approaching the altar on his knees, his arms outstretched'. Greene's own Catholicism influences the characters in many of his novels.

'Tempting the end to come'
'I hadn't the courage for suicide, but it became a habit with me to visit troubled places.' Hence Graham Greene's visits to Mau-Mau Kenya, pre-Castro Cuba, Papa Doc Haiti, war-torn Vietnam, Mexico, Malaya (below)...

Hutchison Library

Fertile partnership
Greene and Carol Reed collaborated to make cinematic history.

Man in Havana, 1958), Haiti under Papa Doc (*The Comedians*, 1966).

Critics are fond of using the joke-geographical term 'Greeneland' to describe the world as seen by Graham Greene – a place even more notable for its seediness and squalor than for its menace and ambiguity. When we read in the first volume of Greene's autobiography, *A Sort of Life* (1971), that 'The first thing I remember is sitting in a pram at the top of a hill with a dead dog at my feet', we know we have entered 'Greeneland'. The writer himself repudiates the term, claiming that he has merely recorded realities (that, for example, there *was* a dead dog); but he has also admitted to having 'a predilection for seedy places' and it would be hard to deny that a writer's approach to the world is a selective one, largely determined by his temperament (and Greene

classifies himself as a manic-depressive!).

However, 20th-century realities increasingly resemble 'Greeneland', for 'Our whole planet since the war has swung into the fog-belt of melodrama'. As a result, a novel such as *The Honorary Consul* (1973), about the kidnapping of a British diplomat by Paraguayan guerrillas, is always in danger of being overtaken by events, and in *The Comedians*, novelistic licence was not required to dramatize Papa Doc's atrocities – 'Impossible to deepen that night'. As early as *The Ministry of Fear* (1943), one of Greene's characters, hiding in an air-raid shelter while London is blitzed, expresses an idea which seems implicit in his work – that 'Tea on the lawn, evensong, croquet' can no longer be regarded as normal and representative: 'This isn't real life any more.'

Ambiguities of motive and double roles

have also become commonplaces, above all in the field of espionage so close to Greene's heart. In *Our Man in Havana* the chief character lives by simply making up information for the benefit of his superiors – a comic if ultimately dangerous practice suggested by Greene's own wartime experience of the authorities' willingness to accept dubious information rather than leave their file-cards blank. By the time he came to write a more sombre spy story, *The Human Factor* (1978), his friend and former superior Kim Philby had been revealed as the most successful double agent of the century, and Greene was able to send his text to Philby in Moscow for informed comment.

SAD HILARITY
Humour has become increasingly important of recent years. If *May We Borrow Your Husband?* (1967) displays 'a sad hilarity', *Travels with my Aunt* (1969) centres on the extravagant, exuberant adventures and reminiscences of Aunt Augusta, probably Greene's greatest comic creation. *Monsignor Quixote* (1982) brings together Catholicism and Communism, the world, the flesh and the spirit, in a bitter-sweet tragi-comedy. Comedy and violence, melodrama and character-development, have been increasingly integrated in Greene's novels, making redundant the earlier distinction between novels and entertainments. But Greene's mellowing is at best relative, as he demonstrated with *Dr Fischer of Geneva* (1980), a savage late fable in which fiendish humiliations and dangers fail to quell human greed and toadying flattery.

For Graham Greene, writing is an indispensible escape from 'the madness, the melancholia, the panic fear which is inherent in the human situation'. Paradoxically, this serves to bring Greene's readers into the very heart of that situation.

Doctor of letters
Cambridge University conferred an honorary doctorate on Greene in 1962. 'I'm a good enough writer', says Greene. 'Better than many. I'm not proud but realistic. I'm not modest either. But I can't place myself among the giants.' Millions of readers and movie-goers, however, would disagree and place him just there.

WORKS·IN OUTLINE

Graham Greene established himself in the 1930s as a writer of political thrillers. A new dimension appeared in *Brighton Rock* (1938), since the principal characters were Catholics who risked not only death but damnation. For some years the religious element remained important. *The Power and the Glory* (1940) dramatized the conflict between religious and purely secular ideals. *The Heart of the Matter* (1948) described a man driven to commit suicide – considered a mortal sin. With *The End of the Affair* (1951) Greene's attention shifted to the interplay between the committed and the uncommitted. Violence haunts *The Quiet American* (1955), a tragedy of good intentions set in Vietnam, *The Comedians* (1966) and *The Honorary Consul* (1973). Meanwhile Greene also produced lighter novels, and the screen version of *The Third Man* (1950) became one of the most popular films ever. Although continuing to produce thrillers and moral fables, Greene has written with much humour recently.

THE POWER AND THE GLORY

✦ 1940 ✦

A dictator in southern Mexico (below) is bent on suppressing the Roman Catholic Church. One priest remains, however. Fond of the bottle and the father of an illegitimate child, the priest escapes to a safe neighbouring state after years on the run. He is horrified to find himself slipping into complacency and selfishness. A fanatical police lieutenant who has been hunting him down finally traps him and the tragi-comic hero dies joylessly, realizing at the end his failure to love humanity. But events in the lives he has touched suggest that the priest has not lived in vain.

Associated British Picture Corp/Kobal Collection

BRIGHTON ROCK

✦ 1938 ✦

Known as 'the boy', Pinkie Brown (above) is the sadistic leader of a Brighton gang. He murders Fred Hale, a journalist, and then finds himself driven to commit one murder after another. When Rose, a 16-year-old waitress, stumbles across vital evidence, Pinkie marries her to disqualify her from testifying against him. Eventually he persuades Rose to join him in a 'suicide pact' which he has every intention of surviving. But he is found out and vitriol, damnation and extraordinary evidence make for a sensational denouement.

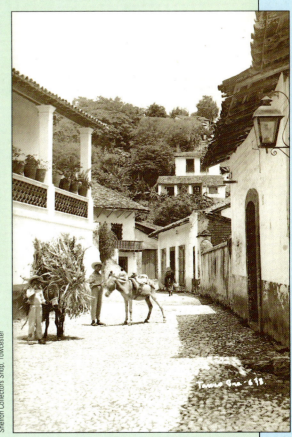

Shelton Collectors Shop, Towcester

93

THE HEART OF THE MATTER
→ 1948 ←

The downfall of Major Henry Scobie (left), deputy commissioner of police, is set against a backdrop of heat, cockroaches and corruption in colonial West Africa. The Major's overwhelming pity for others increasingly compromises his personal and professional life. He borrows money from the unscrupulous Syrian trader Yusef so that his wife Louise can spend some time in South Africa. While she is away, love born of pity involves him with one of the survivors of a U-boat attack, Helen Holt. Louise's unexpected return means that Scobie is torn between two irreconcilable commitments. Moreover, he is blackmailed by Yusef into smuggling diamonds, and his fear of exposure makes him indirectly responsible for the death of his faithful servant Ali. Suicide seems the only way out, but the Major reckons without the detective work of a would-be rival.

Illustrated London News Picture Library

THE THIRD MAN
→ 1950 ←

The promise of a job with his friend and hero Harry Lime (right) lures Rollo Martins to the ruins of occupied Vienna just after World War II. But Lime is dead, knocked down by a speeding car outside his flat. At the funeral Martins encounters Colonel Galloway, a policeman who tells him that Lime was a particularly vile criminal. Martins is determined to prove him wrong. He sets about investigating Harry's death – and discovers that although three men carried the body to the other side of the road, only two of them are accounted for. In his search for 'the third man' Martins sheds many of his former illusions, and the story reaches its thrilling climax with a man-hunt through the sewers of Vienna.

London Films/Kobal Collection

MONSIGNOR QUIXOTE
◆ 1982 ◆

A voyage of discovery through Spain (right) unites Monsignor Quixote and his friend, the Communist ex-mayor Enrique Zancas (Sancho). The monsignor is utterly naive and when he and Sancho go on their travels, Quixote's combination of inexperience and goodness gets them ever deeper into trouble. Trying to blow up a condom (which he believes to be a sort of balloon) in a brothel, hearing a confession in a lavatory, helping an escaped criminal, uncomprehendingly sitting through a pornographic film – Quixote's exploits finally lead to his incarceration as a madman. Sancho comes to the rescue, but, after Quixote's finest exploit, the police pursue them to a monastery where a spectacular glorification awaits Quixote.

Spectrum Colour Library

The Keystone Collection

THE QUIET AMERICAN
◆ 1955 ◆

Vietnam in the fifties (above) was a French colony crumbling under Communist pressure. A battered, middle-aged English journalist, Thomas Fowler, is there trying to remain uncommitted, seeking peace with the opium pipe and in the arms of his Vietnamese mistress, Phuong. His peace is disturbed, however, by the arrival of Alden Pyle, a quiet and serious young American who falls in love with Phuong. Pyle's political activities are equally disruptive, and when he shows no sign of learning from his bloody mistakes, Fowler – though not personally hostile to the American – is forced into action.

MAY WE BORROW YOUR HUSBAND?
◆ 1967 ◆

Honeymooning at a hotel in Antibes, Peter (right) falls prey to the desires of two gay interior decorators, in the title story of this collection of poignantly comic short stories. In *Cheap in August*, Mary Watson takes her first holiday without her husband. Hoping for a fling, she instead finds herself cornered by pathetic old Harry Hickslaughter. In *Mortmain*, Carter finds happiness with Julia – until his old flame begins to persecute the couple with her friendly attentions. And *Two Gentle People* records the few hours during which two middle-aged victims manage to escape marital unhappiness.

Illustrated London News Picture Library

HAITI – NIGHTMARE REPUBLIC

Colonized by Spain and France, occupied by the US and finally terrorized by its own dictators, Haiti bears the scars in the form of widespread poverty, illiteracy and starvation.

Few major authors have embarked on such extensive or adventurous travels as Graham Greene. His visits to far-flung, troubled countries have vividly inspired his most famous writing. One of the most remarkable examples is Haiti, the setting for *The Comedians* – a country with a history of prolonged strife and bloodshed, whose people are even today struggling to establish real democracy.

In December 1492, Christopher Columbus, with a tiny Spanish fleet, landed on the second largest Caribbean island. It was called Aiti – 'mountainous land' – by its indigenous inhabitants, the Arawak Indians, whom Columbus described as 'loveable, tractable, peaceable and praiseworthy'. The Spanish invaders had come for a particular reason: they were looking for gold, which they soon found, on the eastern part of the island.

The 'peaceable' Indians were enslaved by the Spanish invaders and forced to work in the goldmines until near-extinction of the whole tribe. If they managed to survive exhaustion and ill-treatment, they fell victim to diseases imported from Europe, such as smallpox, typhus and influenza. Within 50 years, the native workforce was so depleted that large numbers of African slaves had to be shipped in to replenish the numbers. By now, however, workable gold reserves had become exhausted and the greedy eyes of the conquistadors (Spanish conquerors) had turned to Mexico (1521) and Peru (1532).

FALLING TO THE FRENCH

The Spanish had renamed the island *La Isla Española* (Hispaniola) as it reminded them of home. It remained in Spanish possession, but became a backwater, vulnerable to acquisition by Spain's colonial rivals. In 1586 the city of Santo Domingo was sacked and looted by English forces under Sir Francis Drake, and pirates became increasingly active in the surrounding seas. As Spanish interest in Hispaniola faded, French settlers ensconced themselves on the western part. Their control of this territory, which they named Saint Domingue (the part which today is Haiti), was recognized by the Spanish in 1697.

The French colonists found their 'gold' in the export of sugar, coffee, indigo, cocoa and cotton picked by the slaves. Saint Domingue produced more sugar than all the English Caribbean islands put together, and its overall volume of trade, which required the use of 700 ships, is said to have exceeded that of the thirteen North American colonies. But the planters resented the way in which the mother country creamed off most of the profits. Saint Domingue's sugar had to be refined in French ports and all manufactured goods had to be imported from France. France's stranglehold on Saint Domingue's economic development also encouraged corruption among colonial administrators. For a suitable bribe these officials would turn a blind eye to smuggling, or adjust trading permits causing economic under-development and widespread corruption.

Haiti
This 18th-century map (below) shows Haiti and the focal points of the country's history. Christopher Columbus is seen landing at left, accepting gifts from the natives; slave leader Toussaint L'Ouverture is framed in the lower left corner, and the abolition of slavery is shown centre below.

Jean-Loup Charmet

Labour on tap
The practice of importing African slaves (left) started in the 1520s. Slaves were worked and treated like animals, and when they died were soon replaced. Slavery was to last for more than 250 years, until abolished in 1794.

Jean-Loup Charmet

Jean-Loup Charmet

Mary Evans Picture Library

Slaves uprising
In 1791 the slaves turned against their owners, burning down thousands of coffee estates and sugar plantations. But the death toll was high – 10,000 slaves were killed and 1000 whites. Toussaint L'Ouverture (left), a former slave, joined the struggle and emerged as a brilliant leader.

Caught between the white colonists and the black slaves were their children, mulattos born of white slave-owners and black slave women. In 1791 there were about 28,000 mulattos in Saint Domingue, compared with 40,000 whites and 450,000 blacks. Technically, the mulattos were free and they could own property and even slaves, but apartheid-like measures had been introduced in the 1760s and 1770s to check their influence. Mulattos were, for example, not allowed to marry whites or to reside in France, and certain professions were closed to them. They were also obliged to wear different clothes from whites, to sit in different parts of churches and theatres, and to observe a curfew. Mulatto resentment of such indignities fuelled tensions on the island, but their troubles were slight compared with the appalling treatment that was meted out to the Saint Domingue slaves.

DEATH SENTENCE
Saint Domingue was said to have been 'a mill for crushing negroes as much as for crushing sugar cane'. Any brief description of the conditions endured by the majority of slaves risks being an understatement, for their treatment was nothing less than a protracted death sentence. The slave mortality rate was extremely high, but they were so cheap that their owners, lacking any moral scruples, had no economic incentive to treat them well. Instead of reproducing naturally, the slave population was simply replenished by further shiploads from Africa. The infamous *Code Noir*

King Henri I
Ruler of the north of Haiti from 1807 to 1820, Henri Christophe (inset below) had himself crowned in 1811. He indulged himself in erecting spectacular and extravagant castles around the country, including Sans Souci and Citadelle La Ferrière (below).

laid down regulations for their treatment, stipulating, for example, that after one month's absence a caught runaway slave should have his ears cut off and be branded. A longer absence warranted further mutilation, and capture of a runaway after three months justified his death. Notwithstanding these deterrents, and a huge military presence on the island, some slaves – known as maroons – escaped to freedom in the mountains.

The slaves' one solace was voodoo, a religion rooted in West Africa. Because its practices were not understood by the white masters it was also a valuable means of political communication. In August 1791, a voodoo ceremony in the north of the country gave the signal for a well-organized slave uprising under the leadership of the High Priest Boukman. The slaves murdered many of their white oppressors and burned down the plantations. They took advantage of the general confusion sparked off by the French Revolution: this had left whites and mulattos uncertain about their

Sarah Errington/Hutchison Library

BBC Hulton Picture Library

Sources and Inspiration

Shelton Collectors Shop, Towcester

political rights and the relationship between Saint Domingue and France. The slaves' uprising was to last for twelve years. Boukman was captured and beheaded in its early stages, and then Toussaint L'Ouverture stepped into his place.

Toussaint had been educated by his godfather and taught the medicinal uses of plants by his father, the son of a petty African chieftain who had been captured in war. His skills enabled him to work as a plantation steward, a job normally held by a white man rather than a slave. He was aged about 45 when – despite his privileges – he decided to join the rebels; they seem to have recognized him immediately as their leader. Toussaint perfected the slave army's guerrilla tactics and the art of playing one colonial power off against another. Thus in 1793 he was allied with both Spanish and French royalists. But in 1794, when the French Republic abolished slavery, he reunited with the French revolutionaries to expel the British invaders of Saint Domingue.

LINKS WITH FRANCE

By 1794 Toussaint was acknowledged as the Lieutenant Governor of a colonial state within the French Empire. But after years of war and turmoil it was a predictably authoritarian state. Slavery was replaced by a system of hired labour, and trading arrangements with France became more favourable to the colony. But military men exercised the political power and Toussaint himself controlled government revenue. This was an unhealthy precedent.

Toussaint L'Ouverture trusted in the ideals of the French Revolution. The new Emperor of France, however, Napoleon Bonaparte, was suspicious of Toussaint's independent constitution; and the fabulous profits made in the days of slavery ultimately weighed more with him than the principle of racial equality. In 1801 Napoleon despatched a mammoth French expeditionary force to the Caribbean, and Toussaint, invited to 'negotiate', was ignominiously shipped to France. In 1803, aged about 60, he died of debility and maltreatment in a French prison.

American occupation
Plundered by Spain and France, Haiti finally fell prey to American 'protection'.

Exporting art
Brightly coloured, naive painting has become one of the country's most marketable industries.

When they heard of this treachery, Toussaint's lieutenants, Jean-Jacques Dessalines and Henri Christophe, continued the war for Haiti's independence. With American aid, the hard-fighting rebel army vanquished the French, who had already been weakened by yellow fever. The island's independence was declared on 1 January 1804; it was the world's first Black Republic and given its Indian name, Haiti. But the war of independence was followed by civil war. After Dessalines had proclaimed himself Emperor Jacques I, large numbers of whites were massacred, and many more fled the country; tension mounted between mulatto and black citizens. Dessalines himself was killed trying to suppress a mulatto revolt just two years later.

After Dessalines' death, Haiti was temporarily divided. Henri Christophe established a monarchy in the north and proceeded to build a series of castles, the most spectacular of which is Citadelle La Ferrière, which took thirteen years and – reputedly – the lives of 20,000 workers to build. After King Henri I's suicide this kingdom was re-absorbed into Haiti, whose independence France recognized in 1825, on extremely onerous terms. Ninety million gold francs had to be paid to the former mother country, an impossible sum which Haiti could raise only by loans. In 1844 the eastern part of the island seceded as the Dominican Republic. Haiti's history for the rest of the 19th century was

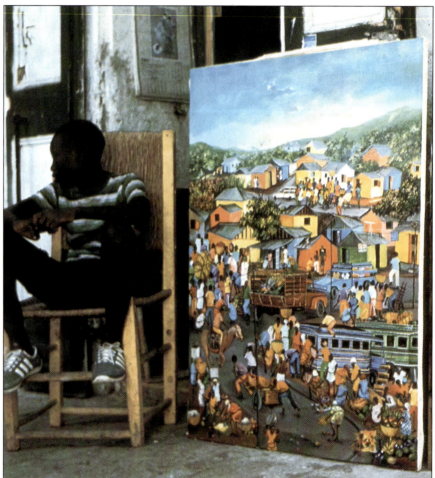

Berlitz Guides/Spectrum Colour Library

Inescapable poverty
(left) Poverty and unemployment are the bleak realities for most of Haiti's population. With the highest illiteracy, infant mortality and starvation rates, the country is the poorest in the Western hemisphere. The average life expectancy is 48 years.

Fear and loathing
The infamous dictator, François Duvalier, known as Papa Doc or Baron Samedi, ruled Haiti with an iron hand – and military backup (right) – from 1957. In 1964 he proclaimed himself Life President, a position he held by reputedly killing tens of thousands of men, women and children until his death in 1971. Even his reign of terror, however, could not suppress the anger of the Haitians (below).

one of constant upheaval, instability and repeated foreign intervention. This, coupled with widespread poverty, particularly in rural areas, led to severe political unrest.

AMERICAN INTERVENTION

Between 1911 and 1915, seven Haitian presidents were overthrown; the last of them, Vilbrun Guillaume Sam, was torn apart by a crowd enraged by a massacre of political prisoners. His death precipitated the American occupation, which lasted from 1915 until 1934. The Americans wished to protect their investments in the railways and ports; and when they left they took the last remaining gold reserves as compensation for Haiti's outstanding debts. Members of the mulatto élite, who

Ruling by force
The 9000 strong Tontons Macoutes propped up Baby Doc's dictatorship, with the assistance of the Army (above), a large presidential guard, and the Leopards – soldiers armed and trained by the US.

had been sponsored by the Americans at the expense of black Haitians, presided over a country disfigured by corruption, violence and, for the vast majority of its citizens, appalling poverty.

Driven from participation in political life, the black middle class – teachers, doctors, lawyers – developed the *Noiriste* movement. This was an affirmation of Haiti's African roots and of voodoo, and it attracted men like Dr François Duvalier, better known as Papa Doc. In 1946 the first black president since the American occupation, Dumarsais Estimé, was elected. He recognized trade unions, and the mulatto aristocracy's monopoly of political power was broken. François Duvalier was a minister in Estimé's government, and was bitterly opposed to Estimé's successor, Colonel Paul Magloire.

Magloire favoured the old mulatto élite, and was backed by the Army, the Roman Catholic Church and the United States. But he was unsuccessful in trying to prolong his term of office, and, in December 1956, he and his family were forced into exile – leaving behind the traditional hallmark of empty coffers. There was chaos in Haiti until the following year, when François Duvalier was elected president. Although his followers intimidated political rivals during the election, Duvalier's victory was genuine, particularly in the rural areas of Haiti.

PAPA DOC AND BABY DOC
Papa Doc was destined to become the most infamous of Haiti's dictators. No one knows exactly how many people were killed during his regime, but estimates run as high as 50,000. In using terror he was not unusual by Haitian standards: what was unusual was its universality and the fact that

Voodoo magic
Baby Doc's face adorns the gate to a voodoo temple (above), symbolizing the marriage of politics and this ancient, primitive religion.

A better tomorrow?
Set in an idyllic location, with miles of golden beaches, an abundance of tropical fruits and breathtaking vistas, Haiti remains a land of contradictions. Perhaps stability lies in the future.

prominent people, foreigners and even members of the president's own family were not exempted.

Papa Doc was determined to stay in power, and after the 1964 election had himself proclaimed President for Life. New prayers were published to give him semi-divine status: 'Our Doc who art in the National Palace for life, hallowed be Thy name by present and future generations. Thy will be done at Port-au-Prince and in the provinces. Give us this day our new Haiti . . .' Papa Doc ruled with the aid of his private police, the Tontons Macoutes, the agents of his reign of terror. Within months they liquidated mulattos who had been unable to flee, and they used their position to extort bribes and pay-offs from ordinary citizens.

In addition to political terror, continuing economic havoc and international disapproval, Haiti at this time suffered catastrophic floods, hurricanes and earthquakes. Under Papa Doc, the state was arguably the poorest and unhappiest in the world. Before his death in 1971, Papa Doc named his son, 19-year-old Jean-Claude, as his successor on the same terms. Nicknamed 'Baby Doc' on account of his chubbiness and youth, Jean-Claude Duvalier began his reign with gestures aimed at conciliating world opinion.

OPPOSITION AND EXILE
With an eye to Western financial support, Baby Doc permitted tokens of political opposition and claimed to have abolished the Tontons Macoutes. In reality, however, Baby Doc's regime was simply more selective and discreet in its repression. But since the regime's image had become more palatable, foreign aid began coming to Haiti. The beneficiaries of this were Baby Doc and the mulatto élite with whom he allied himself by his marriage to Michele Bennett. The wedding was financed with two million dollars of Haitian government funds. By the end of 1985, Haiti boiled over and in February 1986 Baby Doc was forced to seek asylum in France. In keeping with the tradition that has leached wealth from Haiti since its colonial beginnings, he took several hundred million dollars with him into exile.

BIBLIOGRAPHY

Adamson, Judith, *Graham Greene and Cinema.* Pilgrim Books (Norman, 1984)

Aguila, Juan del, *Cuba: Dilemmas of a Revolution.* Westview Press (Boulder, 1984)

Aldington, Richard, *D. H. Lawrence.* Bern Porter (Belfast, 1982)

Allain, Marie-Francoise, *The Other Man: Conversations with Graham Greene.* Simon & Schuster (New York, 1983)

Baker, Ida, *Katherine Mansfield: The Memories of LM.* Salem House Books (Topsfield, 1986)

Balbert, Peter, and Marcus, Philip L., eds., *D. H. Lawrence: A Centenary Consideration.* Cornell University Press (Ithaca, 1985)

Baldwin, Dean R., *H. E. Bates: A Literary Life.* Susquehanna University Press (Cranbury, 1987)

Balsdon, John P., *The Emperor Gaius (Caligula)* (reprint of 1964 edition). Greenwood Press (Westport, 1977)

Bates, Herbert E., *Edward Garnett* (reprint of 1950 edition). Folcroft (Folcroft, 1974)

Becker, George J., *D. H. Lawrence.* Ungar (New York, 1980)

Berdan, Frances, *The Aztecs in Central Mexico: An Imperial Society.* Henry Holt & Co. (New York, 1982)

Black, Michael H., *D. H. Lawrence: The Early Fiction.* Cambridge University Press (New York, 1986)

Cockburn, Claude, *Cockburn Sums Up.* Charles River Books (Boston, 1981)

DeVitis, A. A., *Graham Greene.* G. K. Hall (Boston, 1986)

Erdinast-Vulcan, Daphna, *Graham Greene's Childless Fathers.* St. Martin's Press (New York, 1987)

Foster, Charles R., and Valdman, Albert, eds., *Haiti – Today and Tomorrow.* University Press of America (Lanham, 1985)

Friedman, Melvin J., ed., *Vision Obscured: Perceptions of Some Twentieth-Century Catholic Novelists.* Fordham University Press (Bronx, 1970)

Graves, Robert, *Good-Bye to All That: An Autobiography.* Richard West (Philadelphia, 1980)

Greene, Graham, *Getting to Know the General: The Story of an Involvement.* Simon & Schuster (New York, 1984)

Heyden, Doris, and Villasenor, Luis F., *The Great Temple and the Aztec Gods.* Ocelot Press (Claremont, 1984)

Holderness, B. A., *British Agriculture since 1945.* Longwood (Wolfeboro, 1985)

Keane, Patrick J., *A Wild Civility: Interactions in the Poetry and Thought of Robert Graves.* University of Missouri Press (Columbia, 1980)

Kelley, Richard, *Graham Greene.* Ungar (New York, 1985)

Kenmare, Dallas, *Fire-Bird: A Study of D. H. Lawrence.* Bern Porter (Belfast, 1978)

Kirby, Paul F., *The Autobiography of Hercules.* Bolchazy-Carducci (Oak Park, 1986)

Llerena, Mario, *The Unsuspected Revolution: The Birth and Rise of Castroism.* Cornell University Press (Ithaca, 1978)

Lloyd, Dana O., *Ho Chi Minh.* Chelsea House (Edgemont, 1986)

Mack, John E., *A Prince of Our Disorder: The Life of T. E. Lawrence.* Little, Brown (Boston, 1978)

Mehoke, James S., *Robert Graves: Peace-Weaver.* Mouton de Gruyter (Hawthorne, 1975)

Metraux, Alfred, *Voodoo in Haiti.* Schocken Books (New York, 1972)

Momigliano, Arnaldo, *Claudius, the Emperor and His Achievement* (reprint of 1961 edition). Greenwood Press (Westport, 1981)

Page, Bruce, *The Philby Conspiracy.* Ballantine Books (New York, 1981)

Perowne, Stewart, *Roman Mythology.* Peter Bedrick Books (New York, 1984)

Rodman, Selden, *Haiti: The Black Republic.* Devin-Adair (Greenwich, 1985)

Rudolfo, Anaya A., *Lord of the Dawn: The Legend of Quetzalcoatl.* University of New Mexico Press (Albuquerque, 1987)

Seymour-Smith, Martin, *Robert Graves: His Life and Work.* Henry Holt & Co. (New York, 1983)

Singh, Tajindar, *The Literary Criticism of D. H. Lawrence.* Apt Books (New York, 1984)

Snipes, Katherine, *Robert Graves.* Ungar (New York, 1979)

Weinzinger, Anita, *Graves as a Critic.* Longwood (Wolfeboro, 1982)

Wyatt, Donald, *Aldous Huxley.* Methuen Inc. (New York, 1985)

INDEX

Note Page numbers in italic type refer to illustrations.

A

Across the Bay (Bates) 71, *71*
Aeneid (Virgil) 50
agriculture, 20th century England, mechanization 72-76, *72-76*
Ahuitzotl 28
All Quiet on the Western Front (Remarque) 43
Antigua, Penny, Puce (Graves) 44, 45, 46, *46*
'Aspen, Lydia' of *Love for Lydia* 60, *60-61*, 61, 62, *62-63*, 63, 64, *64*, 65, *65*
'Aspen, Miss Bertie and Miss Juliana' of *Love for Lydia* 60, 64, *65*
'Athenodorus' of *I, Claudius* 37
'Augustus' of *I, Claudius* 36, *36*, 37, 38, 39, 40, 41, *41*, 49, 52
Aztec Indians 24, *24*, 26, *26*, 27, 28, *28*

B

'Banford' of *The Fox* 14, 15, *15*, 16, 17
Barrie, J. M. 54
Bates, Herbert Ernest 53, *53*, *55*, 58, 60, 67, *68*
  art lessons 54
  as clerk in leather factory 54
  as junior reporter 54
  as literary editor of the *Spectator* 58
  as RAF short-story writer *57*, 58, 68
  autobiography 56, 59, 66
  biography of Edward Garnett 59, 66
  birth 54
  career 66-68, *66-68*
  CBE (Commander of the British Empire) 59, *59*
  characters 64-65, *64-65*
  childhood 54, 72, 73, *73*, 74, *75*, 76, *76*
  children 56, 57
  death 59
  description of Rushden, Northamptonshire *54*
  essay on Shakespeare 54
  film adaptations *58*, 59

first novel 66
'Flying Officer X' stories 58, 59, 68, *68*
gardening 57, *57*
ill health 57, 58, 59
key dates 55
marriage 56
radio plays 59
school 54
travels abroad 56, 58, 59
views on short story 66
views on writing 67
visits to London 56
works in outline 69-71, *69-71*
Bates, Lucy 54, *55*
Bates, Marjorie ('Madge') Cox 55, 56, 57, 58, *58*, 59
Bavarian Gentians (Lawrence) 19
Bennett, Arnold 9
Blossoming World, The (Bates) 59
Boukman, High Priest 97, 98
Boy in the Bush, The (Skinner/Lawrence) 10, 18, *19*
Breath of Fresh Air, A (Bates) 59
Brett, Dorothy 10, 11, *11*
Brighton Rock (Greene) 80, 90, 93, *93*
'Brown' of *The Comedians* 84, *84*, 85, *85*, 86, *86*, 87, *87*, 88, *88*, 89
Browning, Robert 90
Burgess, Guy 81
Burrows, Louie 8

C

'Caligula' of *I, Claudius* 36, 38, *38*, 39, *39*, 40, *40*, 41, 50, 51-52
'Calpurnia' of *I, Claudius* 38, *38*, 40, *40*
Cannan, Gilbert 20
Cape (Jonathan) 55, 58, 59, 66
Captain's Doll, The (Lawrence) 20
Castro, Fidel *82*, 83, *91*
Chambers, Edmund 7
Chambers, Jessie 7, *7*, 8
Chambers, Sarah Anne 7
Charlotte's Row (Bates) 69, *69*
Cheap in August (Greene) 95, *95*
Chekhov, Anton Pavlovich 66, *67*
Christophe, Henri 97, 98
Claudius the God (Graves) 45
'Claudius' of *I, Claudius* 35, *35*, 36, 37, *37*, 38, *38*, 39, *39*, 40, *40*, 41, 50, 52

Cockburn, Claude 78
Cohen, Harriet 56
Collected Poems (Graves) 42, *44*
Collected Short Stories (Graves) 47, *47*
Colonel Julian (Bates) 71
Columbus, Christopher 96, *96*
Comedians, The (Greene) 83, 84-89, *84-89*, 92, 93, 96
Confidential Agent, The (Greene) 80, 90
Conrad, Joseph 66
Coppard, A. E. 59
Corke, Helen 8
Cortés, Hernán 28
Count Belisarius (Graves) 44
Cruise of the Breadwinner, The (Bates) *68*

D

D. H. Lawrence, Novelist (Leavis) 20
Daffodil Sky, The (Bates) 71
Darling Buds of May, The (Bates) 59, 68, 69, 70, *70*
Daughters of the Vicar, The (Lawrence) 20
Dawn (Graves) 45
Dax, Alice 8
Depression, The 62, *62*
Dessalines, Jean-Jacques 98
Douglas, Norman 10
Doyle, Sir Arthur Conan 54
Dr Fischer of Geneva (Greene) 92
Drake, Sir Francis 96
Duvalier, François ('Papa Doc') 84, 85, 86, 87, *91*, 92, *99*, 100
Duvalier, Jean-Claude ('Baby Doc') 100, *100*
Duvalier, Michele Bennett 100

EF

Enchantress, The (Bates) 71
End of the Affair, The (Greene) 90, 93
English countryside, 20th century changes 72-76, *72-76*
Escaped Cock, The (Lawrence) 20
Estimé, Dumarsais 100
Fair Stood the Wind for France (Bates) 58, 59, 68, *68*, 69, *69*

Fallen Idol, The (Greene) 80
Fallow Land, The (Bates) 58, 66, *67*, 73
Fenton, Leslie 59
Forster, E. M. 9, 20
Fox, The (Lawrence) 14-15

G

Galsworthy, John 66
Garnett, David 58
Garnett, Edward 18, 19, 20, 56, 58, 59, *59*, 66, 67
'Germanicus' of *I, Claudius* 37, 38, 40
'Gipsy' of *The Virgin and the Gipsy* 12, 13, 16, *16*, 17
Golden Fleece, The (Graves) 44
Goodbye to All That (Graves) 34, 43, 45
Graves, Alfred Perceval 30, *30*, 31
Graves, Amalie von Ranke 30, *30*
Graves, Beryl Hodge 34, *34*, 35, *35*
Graves, Nancy Nicholson 31-32, *32*, 33, 34
Graves, Robert von Ranke 29, *29*, 36, *43*, *44*, 52
  as 'adopted son' of Deyá, Mallorca *35*
  as Professor of Poetry at Oxford 35
  Beryl Hodge and 34, *34*, 35
  birth 30
  career 42-44, *42-44*
  characters 40-41, *40-41*
  childhood 30, *30*, 31
  children 32, 33, 34, *34*
  death 35
  decline of CBE 35
  enlistment in British army 31
  heart problem 31
  in Cairo *32*, 33
  key dates 31
  marriage to Nancy Nicholson 31, *32*
  poetry 32, 33, 34, *34*, 35, 42, 43, 44, 45
  premature obituary 31
  printing press 34, *42*
  relationship with Laura Riding 33, 34, *34*, *42*
  school *30*, 31
  'shamming' of insanity 31
  siblings *30*
  Siegfried Sassoon and 31, *33*
  study of classics 48
  view of himself 35

works in outline 45-47, *45-47*
World War I and 31, *31, 43*
Greek Myths, The (Graves) 35, 52
Greene, Barbara 80
Greene, Charles Henry 78, *79*
Greene, Elizabeth 80
Greene, Henry Graham 77, *77, 78, 83,* 87
  appendicitis 79
  as British intelligence agent 80-81, *80*
  as playwright 82, *91*
  as propagandist for Ruhr Germans 79, *79*
  autobiography 78, 92
  birth 78
  career 90-92, *90-92*
  Catholicism and 79, 82, 90, *91, 92, 93*
  characters 88-89, *88-89*
  childhood 78
  children 79
  film criticism 80, *90*
  film scripts 80, 82, *92, 93*
  honorary doctorate from Cambridge *92*
  jobs 79
  key dates 79
  marriage 79
  move to Antibes 82
  Omar Torrijos and 83, *83*
  Oxford and 78, 79
  'playing' of Russian roulette 79
  poetry 78
  psychoanalysis 78
  public protests against oppression 83
  school 78
  suppression of *Journey Without Maps* 80, *80*
  The Times and 70, 80, *80*
  travels abroad 79, *79,* 80, *80, 81,* 82, *82, 91, 91,* 96
  works in outline 93-95, *93-95*
Greene, Vivien Dayrell-Browning 79
'Grenfel, Henry' of *The Fox* 15, 16, 17
Gun for Sale, A (Greene) 90

H

Haiti 84, *84,* 86, 87, 88, 89, *91,* 92, 96-100, *96-100*
Heart of the Matter, The (Greene) *80,* 81, 90, 93, 94, *94*
Hemingway, Ernest 66
Henri I, King in northern Haiti *see* Christophe, Henri
Ho Chi Minh *82,* 83
Hodge, Alan *35,* 44, 45, 46
'Holland, Nancy' of *Love for Lydia* 62, *62,* 63, 64

'Holland, Tom' of *Love for Lydia* 61, 62, *62,* 63, 64, *65*
Homer 50
Honorary Consul, The (Greene) 92, 93
House of Women, A (Bates) 76
Hueffer, Ford Madox 8
Human Factor, The (Greene) 81, 92
Huxley, Aldous 11

I

I, Claudius (Graves) 34, 35, *35,* 36-41, *36-41,* 44, 45, 49, 50, 51, 52
Iliad (Homer) 50

J

J'Accuse – The Dark Side of Nice (Greene) 83
Jacaranda Tree, The (Bates) 59, 68
Jackson, Schuyler 34
Jacques I, Emperor of Haiti *see* Dessalines, Jean-Jacques
James, Henry 20
'Johnson, Blackie' of *Love for Lydia* 61, *61,* 64, *64-65*
'Jones, Major' of *The Comedians* 84, 85, 86, 87, 88, *88*
'Joseph' of *The Comedians* 84, 88
Journey Without Maps (Greene) 80, *80*
'Julia' of *I, Claudius* 37, 40
Juno 41, 49, 50, *50, 51,* 52, *52*
Jupiter 41, 49, *49,* 50, *50,* 51, 52, *52*

K

Kangaroo (Lawrence) 10, 19, *19*
King Jesus (Graves) 43, 45, 47, *47*
Kipling, Rudyard 54
Korda, Alexander 59, 80, 82, *82*

L

Lady Chatterley's Lover (Lawrence) 11, 13, 18, 19, 21, 23, *23*
Laetitia (Lawrence) 19
Last Poems (Lawrence) 19

Lawless Roads, The (Greene) 80
Lawrence and the Arabs (Graves) 43, *43*
Lawrence, Arthur 6, 7
Lawrence, David Herbert Richards 5, *5,* 7, *20*
  as clerk 7
  as illustrator *20*
  as teacher 7
  birth 6
  burial 11, *11*
  career 18-20, *18-20*
  censorship of 9, 13, *19*
  characters 16-17, *16-17*
  death 11
  education 6, 7, *7*
  Edward Garnett and 66
  ill health 7, 8, 9, 11, 18
  introduction to London literary life 8
  key dates 7
  marriage 8
  pseudonym 18
  Robert Graves' views on 43
  seizure of paintings by London police 11, 13
  travels abroad 8, *8-9,* 9-10, 19, *19*
  views on Mexico 24, *24,* 25, 26, *26,* 28
  views on New Mexico 10, *11*
  views on writing 12, 18
  works in outline 21-23, *21-23*
  World War I and 9, *9,* 18
Lawrence, Frieda von Richthofen Weekley 8, *8,* 9, 10, 11, *11,* 18, *18,* 19, *19,* 20
Lawrence, Lydia 6, 7, *7,* 8
Lawrence, T. E. (Lawrence of Arabia) 43, *43,* 45, 56
Lean, David 59, 68
Leavis, F. R. 20
'Lime, Harry' of *The Third Man* 94, *94*
'Livia' of *I, Claudius* 36, *36,* 37, 38, 39, 40, 41, *41*
Living Room, The (Greene) 91
Long Weekend, The (Graves/Hodge) 44, 45, 46, *46*
Loser Takes All (Greene) 82
Love for Lydia (Bates) 59, 60-65, *60-65,* 68, 71, 72, 75, 76
Luhan, Tony 11

M

Mackenzie, Compton 10, 20
Maclean, Donald 81
'Magiot, Doctor' of *The Comedians* 85, 87, 88, *88*
Magloire, Paul 100
Mallorca 34, *34,* 35, *35, 42,* 44, 47

Man Within, The (Greene) 79
Mansfield, Katherine 8, *8*
'March' of *The Fox* 14, 15, *15,* 16, *17*
Marsh, Edward 9, 42
Masefield, John 32
May We Borrow Your Husband? (Greene) 92, 95, *95*
Mayan Indians 24, *24,* 25, *25*
'Medullina' of *I, Claudius* 37
Metamorphoses, The (Ovid) 49
Mexico 10, 11, 13, *14, 20,* 23, 24-28, *24-28*
Mill, The (Bates) 58
Miller, Henry 69
Milton, John 43, 54
Ministry of Fear, The (Greene) 92
Monsignor Quixote (Greene) 92, 95, *95*
Mornings in Mexico (Lawrence) 26
Morrell, Lady Ottoline 9, *19*
Mortmain (Greene) 95, *95*
Movements in Modern History (Lawrence) 18
Mr Noon (Lawrence) 18
Mrs Eglantine (Bates) 71
Murry, John Middleton 8, *8,* 9, *10*
Myconian, The (Graves) 47

NO

Napoleon Bonaparte 98
Nazarene Gospel Restored, The (Graves) 43
Our Man in Havana (Greene) 91-92
Ovid 49

P

Paul Morel (Lawrence) 19
Peck, Gregory *58,* 59
Phibbs, Geoffrey 33, 34
Phibbs, Norah 33
Philby, Kim 81, *81,* 92
'Philipot junior' of *The Comedians* 85, 86, 87
Pier-Glass, The (Graves) 45, *45*
'Pineda, Angel' of *The Comedians* 84, 85, 88, 89
'Pineda, Martha' of *The Comedians* 84, 85, *85,* 86, 87, 88, *89*
Plumed Serpent, The (Lawrence) 10, 11, 19, 20, *20,* 21, 23, *23,* 24, 28
Poacher, The (Bates) 66, 76
Portman, Eric *91*
'Postumus' of *I, Claudius* 37, 38, 40
Power and the Glory, The (Greene) 80, 90, 93, *93*

Priestley, J. B. 80
Proceed, Sergeant Lamb (Graves) 44
Prussian Officer, The (Lawrence) 20
Purple Plain, The (Bates) *58,* 59, 68, *68*

Q

Quetzalcoatl, the Plumed Serpent 24, *24,* 25, 26, *27,* 28
Quiet American, The (Greene) 91, 93, *94-95,* 95

R

Rainbow, The (Lawrence) 9, 13, 18, 19, 20, 21, 22, *22*
Ravagli, Angelo 8
Reader over Your Shoulder, The (Graves/Hodge) 44
Reed, Carol *92*
Reproach (Graves) 45
'Richardson' of *Love for Lydia* 60, *60-61,* 61, 62, *62-63,* 63, 64, *64,* 65
Richmond, Kenneth 78
Richthofen, Manfred von 8
Riding, Laura *32,* 33, *33,* 34, *34, 42*
Rivera, Diego *26-27*
Roman gods and heroes 48-52, *48-52*

Russell, Bertrand 9, *19*

S

'Sanderson, Alex' of *Love for Lydia* 61, 62, 63, 64, *64*
Sandinistas 83, *83*
Sassoon, Siegfried 31, *33*
Scarlet Sword, The (Bates) 68, 69, 70, *70*
Sea and Sardinia (Lawrence) 19
Second-Fated, The (Graves) 35
Sergeant Lamb of the Ninth (Graves) 44
Seven by Five (Bates) 71, *71*
Ship of Death, The (Lawrence) 19
Shout, The (Graves) 44
Sisters, The (Lawrence) 19
Skinner, Mollie 10, 18
Slavery 96, *96,* 97, *97,* 98
Sleepless Moon, The (Bates) 59
'Smith, Mr and Mrs' of *The Comedians* 84, *85, 86,* 87, 88, 89
Somoza Debayle, Anastasio 83, *83*
Sons and Lovers (Lawrence) 6, 7, 8, 19, 21, *21*
Sort of Life, A (Greene) 92
Spella Ho (Bates) 58, 76
Stamboul Train (Greene) 80, 90, *90*
Sterne, Mabel Dodge 10, 11, *11*
Studies in Classic American Literature (Lawrence) 18
'Sybil, The' of *I, Claudius* 36, 37, 39

T

Temple, Shirley 80, *90*
They Hanged My Saintly Billy (Graves) 44
Third Man, The (Greene) 80, 81, 93, 94, *94*
'Tiberius' of *I, Claudius* 36, 37, 38, 39, 40, 41
Tick of the Clock, The (Greene) 78
Toast to Ava Gardner, A (Graves) 47
Tolstoy, Leo 67
Tontons Macoutes 84, *84,* 85, *86,* 89, 100, *100*
Torrijos Herrera, Omar 83, *83*
Toussaint L'Ouverture *96,* 97, 98
Travels with my Aunt (Greene) 92
Triple Echo, The (Bates) 59, 68, 69, 71, *71*
Tutin, Dorothy *91*
Twentieth Century-Fox *90*
Two Gentle People (Greene) 95, *95*
Two Sisters, The (Bates) 55, 56, 66, 67

V

Vanished World, The (Bates) 59, 72, 73, 76
Vestal Virgins 37, *37,* 51
Virgil 50

Virgin and the Gipsy, The (Lawrence) 12, 13, 16, *16,* 20
Voodoo 87, *87,* 89, 97, 100, *100*
Voyagers, The (Bates) 56

W

Walpole, Hugh 20
Watkins-Pitchford, D. J. ("BB") 72
Wedding Ring, The (Lawrence) 19
Weekley, Ernest 8
Wells, H. G. 11
White Goddess, The (Graves) 35, 43, 45, 47, *47*
White Peacock, The (Lawrence) 8, 19, 21, *21*
Wife to Mr Milton (Graves) 44
Woman Who Rode Away, The (Lawrence) 11, 13-14, *14,* 16, *16,* 20, 25, 26
Women in Love (Lawrence) 13, 18, 19, 21, 22, *22*
World in Ripeness, The (Bates) 59
World War I 9, 18, 23, 31, 43, *43,* 45, 46, 73, 79
World War II 42, 58, 68, *68,* 69, 71, *76,* 80, 81

Y

'Yvette' of *The Virgin and the Gipsy* 12, *12-13,* 13, 16, *16,* 17, *17*